Pauline D'Alvigny Campbell

Civil War Nurse

(Her Life and Times of War in Atlanta)

Enjoy!
Julie Clarke
Rick Clarke

By Julie Clarke and Edited by Rick Clarke

Dedicated to the memory of Tom & Jimmy Clarke

ISBN: 978-1-7326606-0-1

Printed by Trinity Press, Norcross, Georgia, 2nd printing Oct. 2018

Table of Contents:

INTRODUCTION

Many times I've strolled through the grounds, gazing at the Oak trees, winding my way along the paths, viewing the flowers and stones, or stopping to take a picture. Atlanta's Oakland cemetery is now very familiar to me, more so than the day many years ago, shortly after Rick and I were married, when we attended "Sunday in the Park" and saw Franklin Garrett, the Atlanta historian. Mr. Garrett had made a special appearance that day, sitting under one of the trees, to meet and talk to visitors in a setting that is more like a park than a cemetery. He knows all about who the Oakland volunteers call "residents". In fact, my husband's fourth Great-Grandfather is a "resident" of Oakland who lived in the Victorian era and was one of Atlanta's pioneers. That day Mr. Garrett told Rick, "You come from a family of VERY FINE citizens of Atlanta", in that long slow southern drawl of his. He also confirmed to us that Rick's ancestor, Dr. Peter Paul Noel D'Alvigny, was the role model for Dr. Meade in *Gone with the Wind*. In fact Margaret Mitchell, the author, is also buried here, along with other famous Atlantans, such as the golfer Bobby Jones. From golf balls to cannon balls, or Southern belles to the Bell Tower in Oakland, it's definitely a historical place with a past that I hope to bring back to life in this book.

In olden times people would picnic at their family's graves. At every "Sunday in the Park" event, which typically occurs the first Sunday of October, Rick and I set up a table at the D'Alvigny gravesite and meet and talk with people about the family and Atlanta during the Civil War. There is one point in the cemetery, on a hill near the Bell Tower, where Confederate General John Bell Hood took a position to view the Battle of Atlanta in 1864. Dr. D'Alvigny was nearby, as he was a surgeon at the Atlanta Medical college hospital. He tended the wounded soldiers brought in by train in addition to those from the surrounding area. As a doctor he treated both Union and Confederate soldiers, and citizens, both slave and free. He had a daughter, Pauline, who was also in the city and assisted him.

One year, a lady stopped by our table at the cemetery and we were surprised to learn that she knew all about Pauline. She had seen her picture in a museum in Barnesville, Georgia. Rick and I had never heard of such, and set out one day to find more information on the D'Alvigny family, including Pauline. We continued our genealogical research over the years, which at times involved visiting some of the places where Pauline lived or stayed. Then, at the Atlanta History Center, we found a little known scrapbook of the Women's Pioneer society, which contained Pauline D'Alvigny Campbell's actual account. Therefore, I've set out to present her personal Account which has not been published since her lifetime, and also some accounts of neighbors and friends who were in close proximity to Pauline and her family during the War.

This book is arranged in segments, which takes you chronologically through the life of Pauline, her family and friends, regarding their whereabouts before, during and after, what the South knew as "The War Between the States", which is commonly known now as the "Civil War".

In today's world we realize the evilness of slavery. Even in those days there were Union sympathizers living in Atlanta. However, this is written about a woman, her family and friends from a different time and perspective, a time of war and division of the nation. It is about trying times of raising a family with no father around, little food to eat and a husband that may not return. It is about the dangers of being in the midst of total war for all involved. It is from the Southern perspective and it is about survival.

Starting with her parent's background, I've grouped the Headings by either decade or by year. Pauline's husband was a soldier with Leyden's artillery, so I've included an account from one of his comrades James McMurtrey, and accounts from a friend and neighbor of Pauline, Elizabeth Huff and her daughter Sarah. Pauline's actual words will be identified next to her name in bold letters throughout the book. Also, I've included, by the headings of "Clarke" (my last name) experiences in my own life, when I've travelled or visited the places mentioned by Pauline or major historical events. Many are from vacations or re-enactments that Rick and I took or research trips, but some are just simply from times in my life that coincide with Pauline's.

Pauline came from a deeply religious family. She and many others of the South would be turning to God, the Bible and prayer during the difficult time of War. Therefore, I've included a passage of scripture at the beginning of each chapter that pertains to the content of the chapter.

You will learn how Pauline's wit, wisdom and courage, helped her survive a time when our nation was torn apart. Her home was under attack, she had to care for her children during it all, and help those who needed her. Pauline D'Alvigny Campbell had many roles in her life– Mother, Wife, Daughter, Sister, Matron, Nurse, Neighbor and Friend, and to sum it up – a role that she did not ask for, but was given to her by her community - Heroine.

Julie Clarke

Acknowledgements

I would first like to thank God, for his mercy and guidance. Next, I would like to thank my husband, Rick, who has been a God-send to me. He helped and supported me immensely with my first book, as editor, co-writer and historical advisor. His legacy is so fascinating, it has been a pleasure to research and learn about his ancestry. Next shout-out is to my family and friends and church members, who have offered their opinions and support even when I've cancelled appointments and delayed contact in my efforts to get out this book.

When Rick found the Christian writers group, the *Scribblers*, I didn't realize how involved we would become, and how well we would fit in and the friends we would meet. This group is one of the main reasons that I have a book being published at all. Their tips, opinions and guidance have been invaluable.

Also in doing research, thanks to the resources of the Atlanta History Center, Emory (which was formed from the Atlanta Medical college of long ago which this book is about), Shanna English of the Old Jail museum in Barnesville, David Moore and others of the Oakland Cemetery foundation, the historian from the Stately Oaks in Jonesboro, and our fellow re-enactors including Marie Walker, who portrays a nurse, and continues to inspire us daily with her blogs and adventures. Plus my co-workers Bob Gravlee who helped me in his spare time with a photo that is now on the cover, and Ron Starner, who offered his time and tips with his vast experience in publishing. Also, thanks to all the authors whom we've met and heard speak and gave us tips. Thanks again!

In the close up map below, the Atlanta medical college is marked as a dark square box at the corner of Butler and Jenkins Street (far right).

To the west (left) is the African Church hospital

Below 2 blocks on Butler and Gilmer is D'Alvigny's earliest resident in 1850.

Close up Ambrose Bierce Map 1864

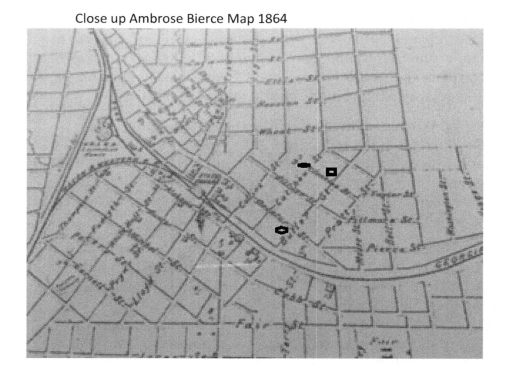

Ambrose Bierce Map 1864 Courtesy Library of Congress

ATLANTA

Scale of 1 Foot
Scale 4 inches to 1 mile

From Vincent's Subdivision Map, published by the City Council

INDEX:

STATE DEPOTS, General Passenger Depot
A W.&A.R.R. Freight Warehouse
B   "   "   Engine House
C A.&W.R.R. Freight Warehouse
D M.&W.R.R. Passenger Depot
E M.&W.R.R. Freight Warehouse
F La Grange   "   "
G Episcopal Church and Parsonage
H Presbyterian Church

1 Baptist Church
2 M. Methodist G. P. Parsonage
3   "   "   "   "
4 Methodist Episcopal Church
5 Methodist   "   "
6 Franklin Church
7 High School
8 Church School
9 Haggard's Seminary

10 Car Factory
11 Arsenal
12 Thompson's Hotel
13 Atlanta   "
14 City   "
15 Market House
16 Guard House
17 Steam Mill
18 Bank

Drawn and printed at Top'l Eng'r Office, H'd'q'rs A.C., in the field, July 23rd 1864.

Chapter 1: Charleston:
Churches and Consumption

"…built upon the foundation of the apostles and prophets, Jesus Christ himself being the chief corner stone." Ephesians 2:20 (KJV)

Look-out!! A cannon ball was heading straight towards a little girl. The massive round ball came from a battle in Atlanta called Ezra Church in the Civil War. Then, I motioned to the little boy who had attempted to pick up the 10 pound ball, rolling it right towards his younger sister. My husband Rick and I were at a "Living History" event at a local historical farm. The solid cannon ball came from Rick's aunt's yard, found many years ago. Luckily, the boy and girl were not hurt, but it reminded me of some of the "close calls" that my husband's ancestor, Pauline D'Alvigny Campbell, had with her three small children in 1864. In the pages ahead, a story will unravel about narrow escapes and matters of life and death. One of the true stories involves her father, Dr. D'Alvigny, Solomon Luckie, an African American barber, and a lamppost that was lit at the premiere of *Gone with the Wind* in Atlanta. It includes her story, in her own words of survival as a civilian and nurse during a horrific time in history. The story of Pauline begins in Charleston, South Carolina.

Clarke: 1998: "The Church's One Foundation"

Upon gazing up at the towering steeple of Saint Patrick's church, the orange-red bricks stood stark against the blue Charleston sky. Could this be the church that was built over Emeline Montzigot De La Foy D'Alvigny's grave? In the stifling heat of August of 1998, my husband Rick and I were vacationing in historic South Carolina. While there we sought-out the

1

known and unknown places where Rick's ancestors, the D'Alvigny's, lived in the eighteen thirties and forties, over one hundred and sixty years ago.

Rick had a look of pure elation with his squinting bluish eyes peering from under his baseball cap, up at the steeple, and then darting back down to three massive brown doors standing boldly in front of the tall Gothic-style church behind the black iron fence. As we were approaching the church, naturally, I was following him, as I usually do, a few steps behind. Rick is much taller than me and it takes extra strides for me to catch up with him. Having circled the church, we noticed the small cemetery in the back, out basking in the sun-light in the cropped green grass.

Earlier, we had read about this church in a book at the local genealogy library on Roman Catholic burials, which listed Emeline D'Alvigny as being buried here February 1849.[1] Supposedly, this was the church the D'Alvigny family attended: Noel, his wife Emeline and their two children, Pauline and Charles who were both born in Charleston. We heard from Rick's relatives that a church was built over Emeline's grave, and we wondered how could this be?

In lieu of our doubts we scoured the entire cemetery for any sign of the name D'Alvigny, but our search was in vain. Not a single D'Alvigny grave was found. There was a small side door to the church, next to the gravesite. We opened the door and stepped inside, sheepishly, finding our way to the church office. With aide of the helpful parish staff, we found several old large ledgers of deaths, baptisms and other church records and began pouring over them with our eyes. We could not find any

---

[1] Susan King, *Roman Catholic deaths in Charleston, South Carolina 1800-1860* (Columbia, S.C. SCMAR) 68

evidence of a D'Alvigny burial at all. We began to wonder, "Were we at the right church"?

The building we were occupying is at the southeast corner of Radcliffe and St. Phillips streets, but it was not the original church that was built in 1838 on Saint Patrick's Day when the cornerstone was first laid. A cemetery first occupied the space purchased ten years earlier by Bishop John England, with hopes to eventually have a church built on the grounds. The original wooden church was a small 50 by 36 feet by 24 feet high structure which was later moved across the street on the southwest corner in 1884 to build a larger sanctuary (where the towering church we just entered now resides adjacent to the cemetery).[2] The original parish had over fifty families in its congregation, including African-Americans.[3] We concluded that the second church was built over Emeline's grave, but we can only surmise. No mention of it was made in the records we viewed. However, another shocking and sad discovery was made in the process of turning the tattered pages of the antique books. Apparently, Noel and Emeline had at least five children while living in Charleston, as the baptisms and subsequent deaths of Eugenie, Louisa and Charlotte were revealed.[4] Pauline and her brother Charles were the only D'Alvigny children that survived beyond the age of three years old.

---

[2] "About Our Parish, a History of St. Patrick Catholic Church", Charleston, SC
http://www.stpatrickcharleston.org/parish-life/about
[3] Susan King, Roman Catholic Deaths...ibid. p. iii
[4] St. Patrick's church Charleston Burial and Baptism records as corroborated by George Raffalovich, "As a Reed with the Reeds (Dr. Noel Pierre-Paul d'Alvigny-1800-1877)" (Historical Collections Health Sciences Library Emory University) 2A.

D'Alvigny: 1830's France to America

Dr. D'Alvigny and his new young bride, Emeline, arrived in Charleston, SC in 1835.[5] It was this beautiful coastal city where they had moved after their marriage in New Jersey to start a family. Charleston was most likely a city close to Noel's heart as it was flourishing with French influence. The Protestant Huguenots had flocked there, escaping religious persecution in the 16th and 17th centuries.[6] However, Noel and Emeline were from French Catholic aristocratic families who, according to family historical accounts, would be no stranger to persecution. Their families had known persecution of another kind, the threat of the guillotine, during the "Reign of Terror" during the French Revolution in the late 1700's. According to family stories, Noel's parents were taken prisoner, perhaps even sent to the Bastille, but were released the very day when Robespierre, the leader of the movement, lost power and was executed.[7]

Pierre Paul Noel d'Alvigny was born in Paris, France on April 13, 1800, and witnessed the exciting return of Napoleon during the 100 days and Battle of Waterloo. The brave fifteen year old boy was likely a surgeon's apprentice during the battle, when Napoleon returned from Exile, and sought to conquer the world in 1815. After Napoleon was defeated, Noel became a soldier in the French Army and fought in several battles around Europe, ultimately becoming a surgeon.[8]

Family lore tells that Noel was forced to make a choice: prison or America, so wisely, he chose the latter. Being listed in the manifest of the ship the Formosa, in April of 1834 from LeHavre, France, he headed for the Americas. As evidenced by some family members, he brought mementos of his life in Paris

---

[5] Raffalovich, As a Reed..Ibid. p. 2A
[6] www.britannica.com/topic/Huguenot; "The Editors of Encyclopedia Britannica" article of 1998
[7] "Raffalovich, "As a Reed"..ibid p. 3
[8] Raffalovich, Ibid. p. 3

with him: a medal of the French Legion d'Honneur (Honor) Chevalier (Knight), supposedly presented to him by Napoleon himself for services at Waterloo, and a bronze French dagger, probably contained in one of three large chests he carried with him on the ship.[9]

I wonder if there was a time when Dr. Noel showed his medals and dagger to Charles and Pauline, who probably looked at them with fascination. What were those stories behind them? Here's what I learned in the following account.

Clarke: 2002: Cloak and Dagger

At a family reunion, one of Rick's newly found relatives, noticed my intrigue and fascination with a dagger that had been passed down that he had brought to display. I know that I was smiling ear to ear when he loaned it to me to help him discover its origination and worth. The dagger was very ornate, and since D'Alvigny was a Mason, I suspected that's where it had come from, some Masonic Lodge either in America or France. I couldn't wait to don a Sherlockian "cloak" with dagger in hand, to figure this mystery out. I had many questions. How old is the dagger? How was it given to Noel? Was this dagger from the Civil War days or from France? So, I set out to find the answers. In the words of the great detective, "The game is afoot"![10]

My first stop was the internet, in my spare time, to figure out when and where the next travelling antique appraisal show was being held, a very popular TV show at the time. Unfortunately, they were on hiatus and there was very little activity nearby. On the internet, I looked up some Masonic

---

[9] Castle Garden, The Batter, http://www.castlegarden.org– Ship manifest of "The Formosa" from LaHavre France to New York April 1834

[10] Arthur Conan Doyle, "The Adventures of Sherlock Holmes" common saying of main character, Sherlock Holmes

daggers online, and they looked similar, but not quite the same, so that was ruled out.

Rick and I are members of the Atlanta History center, so I set up a meeting with the curator and Civil War expert there. He examined the dagger and its accompanying scabbard (cover) with the conclusion that the scabbard had post-dated the dagger, and only the scabbard may have been produced during the Civil War – but he did not know the origin or date of the actual dagger. However, he could say it was not a Civil War dagger. I thanked him for showing me the various swords and daggers in the back storage area, and went on my way.

The next stop was the High Museum of Art, where a sculpture called "The Shade" by the Parisian artist Rodin, sits on the lawn. It was given to the museum from France as a memorial of a fatal airline crash (called Orly) in Paris in 1962 where over 100 people from Atlanta perished. They were there touring Europe, and most of them being Arts supporters and leaders, with their families, and high hopes to make Atlanta a cultural center of the South, sponsored by the Atlanta Art Association. The new Mayor of Atlanta, Ivan Allen flew to Paris to help with the recovery efforts.[11] Also, the Mayor of Buckhead was on the Arts council at the time[12]. It was a shock to the whole city. Rising up again, four years later, Atlanta raised the money to establish an Arts hub. This gave birth to the High Museum of

---

[11] New Georgia Encyclopedia, "Orly Air Crash"
https://www.georgiaencyclopedia.org/articles/history-archaeology/orly-air-crash-1962. Donald R. Rooney, Atlanta History Center, edited by 12/09/2003. Last edited by NGE Staff on 8/1/2017.
https://www.georgiaencyclopedia.org/articles/government-politics/ivan-allen-jr-1911-2003 Note. Mayor Ivan Allen Jr. was married to Louise Richardson, granddaughter of Hugh T. Inman.

[12] Dan Whisenhunt, post on May 4, 2012
https://www.reporternewspapers.net/2012/05/04/50-years-later-orly-a-painful-memory/

Art, and other local cultural icons included in the current Art mecca of Atlanta.

Passing the museum, I made my way to the huge theater, where they were appraising items that day. I paid a small fee and sat in one of the seats, awaiting my turn. I wasn't sure they would know about a dagger, or if it even qualified as "Art", but I was fast running out of options. Hopefully, I would get a French War aficionado to examine my artifact. It was a very long day, as a bunch of people sat for hours waiting to be called. And as it goes, I was among the last few to be called forth. When it was my turn, I proudly handed the man in front of me the dagger, telling him, "I believe this dagger pre-dates the Civil War, but am not quite sure of its origin". I also mentioned it belonged to my husband's French ancestor, who was a Civil War surgeon, as told to Rick by his grandmother Mildred. He took it in his hands, turning it back and forth, looking at the intricate engravings. Then, suddenly, both of our eyes plummeted downward. I couldn't believe it – He dropped it! He then reached down to retrieve it, but the deed had been done. I don't know what the look on my face was, as this wasn't even my dagger to begin with. He then proceeded to tell me, late 1800's, and it does not pre-date the Civil War. I couldn't quite believe that. Stunned by his response and upset with his clumsiness, I exasperatingly took the dagger he returned to me and left.

I did not give up. There were a few numbers on the dagger, barely visible, but the month "July" was clear. I didn't know the year - only the numbers 27, 28, 29. My continuous search on the internet, focusing on French history, finally yielded me a result "The Three Glorious Days" of July in 1830, which was a very short Revolution in France that ousted Charles X from the throne. The dates of the rebellion were 27th, 28th and 29th. "Elementary, My Dear Watson"!

D'Alvigny: 1830-1840's Truly A Best Friend

Pierre P. Noel D'Alvigny was starting over in a new country. Did he leave a family behind as he started his life with Emeline in Charleston? We may never know all of the answers. Perhaps he thought gone were the days of rebellion, maybe more glorious days were to come. Not one of us can know the future. He sought to find that which was his calling in France, and what was familiar to him – being a doctor, mason and soldier.

Noel D'Alvigny joined the Masonic Lodge in Charleston, and family stories mention that he sought their help initially. It was rare for a Catholic to also be a Mason, as this was frowned upon by the church and many Masons were excommunicated for this reason during this time.[13] The D'Alvigny's had kept close ties to the Roman Catholic Church despite Noel's Masonic ties.

Before marrying Emeline De La Foy in Woodbridge New Jersey, Noel lived in New York and earned a doctorate degree at the University of Indiana in New Albany. Since Emeline's father was Jean Baptiste Monzigot De La Foy, per family records, an Army Captain during Napoleon's reign, it is likely Noel knew of the Foy family while in France.[14]

Once back in Charleston, Noel and his family lived on the west side of town, now known as Antique Row. They resided on King Street where Dr. D'Alvigny set up practice as a dentist. One night in 1838, before nine o'clock, on April 27th a paint store on King Street caught fire. Bells were ringing loudly. Chaos hit the city as the all-consuming fire quickly spread encompassing 150 acres. Tragically, people died and homes, businesses and churches were consumed in flames and burned to the ground. The Charleston Hotel had just been victim to a fire the previous

---

[13] Raffalovich, As a Reed With the Reeds" Appendix IV "Dalvigny as a Mason"
[14] Records from Charles D'Alvigny descendants

year, and was destroyed once again.[15] It is not known whether the D'Alvigny's home was affected, but their community was certainly devastated. As the bells rang out, the D'Alvigny's more than likely feared their home may succumb to the fiery red flames around them heading up Second Street. Emeline would have known by now that she was pregnant with Pauline, joyful and fearful at the same time, elated yet still grieving the loss of the first baby that died less than a year earlier. Pauline was born in October of 1838, six months after the fire. Her brother Charles would be born five years later.

The town of Charleston was becoming more and more the leading city of the South, every year with inventions and progress. In 1839, a French observer noted that Americans had "mania" regarding the subject of railroads. The nearby town of Branchville, between Charleston and Columbia, claimed to be the "first railroad junction" in the world. Charleston did hold claim to having the first passenger train, called the "Best Friend of Charleston". Unfortunately a boiler engine exploded and the train became inoperable less than 6 months after its inaugural run on Christmas day 1830. Later parts were used to build another engine called the "Phoenix".[16]

When you talk about having a best friend that would do anything for you, for Emeline D'Alvigny that friend was Caroline Crovatte Reed. When Emeline's children were born, she and Noel chose Caroline to be their Godmother. She had met Caroline, a young widow with no children and a patient of Dr. D'Alvigny. Caroline had moved to Charleston from up north since marrying George Reed, the Captain of a Tramp steamer ship in Boston Mass. Shortly after their wedding they set sail on the high seas off the coast. How exciting that must have been for Caroline, a new bride on an adventure with her new husband

---

[15] https://thetandd.com/lifestyles/great-fire-of-destroyed-at-least-a-quarter-of-charleston/article_641d0f19-b92c-5cd9-b3bf-7b44c646fd9e.html From the "Times and Democrat" online news site article "Great Fire of 1838 destroyed at least a quarter of Charleston "Courtesy of the South Carolina Historical Society, May 3, 2018

[16] (http://www.carolana.com/SC/Transportation/railroads/home.html)

to begin their life together. Sadly, tragedy hit the newlyweds, and George died and was buried at sea. The distraught bride found her way to Charleston, South Carolina and to the home of the D'Alvigny's.[17] She lived with them and helped with the children, as Emeline became very sick.

When Pauline was just eleven years old and Charles only six, their mother Emeline succumbed to Consumption, which we know today as Tuberculosis. She passed away in February of 1849 at the age of thirty-four years. As mentioned earlier, St. Patrick's Church was moved and rebuilt, and we believe it now resides over her grave and probably those of her three children.

Shortly after his wife's death, Dr. Noel married the lovely Caroline, as it had been the wishes of Emeline.[18] Both Pauline and Charles adored Caroline, who was already like a mother to them. While passing the familiar sights of the glorious South Carolina homes with the wide piazzas and beautiful wrought iron gates, the D'Alvigny family would likely have boarded the local train to take a new passage. As the children would gaze out the window as the train rambled along, they would see the blur of the trees and vegetation. The family would be leaving behind joys and tragedies of their former life. They were rising out of Charleston fires, sickness and loss, travelling to a new home in Atlanta, which was also known as the "Gate City". Not knowing that, at one point in the future, Atlanta would also be rising as they were now, as a Phoenix from the ashes.[19]

---

[17] Raffolivich, "As a Reed" ibid 2 and family papers

[18] Sarah Huff, "Mrs Robert Campbell A Heroine of the Hospital", provided by Old Jail Museum & Archives, Barnesville Georgia - dated July 4th 1923 3

[19] Definition of Phoenix: https://en.wikipedia.org/wiki/Phoenix_(mythology) In Greek mythology, a phoenix is a long-lived bird that cyclically regenerates or is otherwise born again.. Associated with the Sun, a phoenix obtains new life by arising from the ashes of its predecessor.

Saint Patrick's Catholic Church, Charleston, SC, 1998,
photo by Julie Clarke

Dagger and Scabbard of Noel D'Alvigny. Engraved with the dates of the July 27, 28, 29 of 1830 and text "Liberte et un Force"[20]-

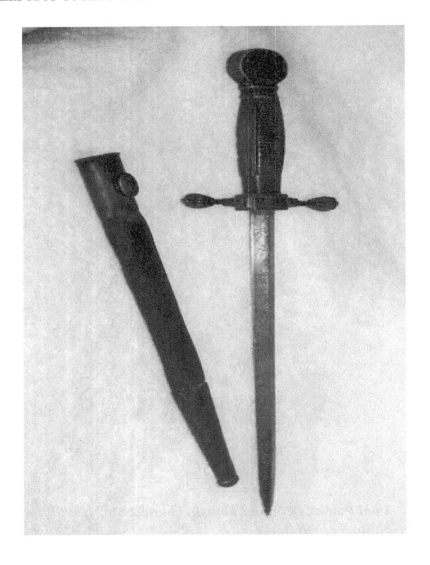

---

[20] Google Translate   Freedom and a Force" (photo by Julie)

Caroline Mary Crovatte Reed D'Alvigny
Spouse of Dr. P.P. Noel D'Alvigny, and
Stepmother to Charles and Pauline D'Alvigny
(photograph is courtesy of Wood family)

Pauline D'Alvigny Campbell – Civil War Nurse

Chapter 2: "He Leadeth Thee"

"Thus saith the Lord, thy Redeemer, the Holy One of Israel; I am the Lord thy God which teacheth thee to profit, which leadeth thee by the way that thou shouldest go".   Isaiah 48:17 (KJV)

D'Alvigny: 1850s: Atlanta: From Iron Gates to Gate City

Upon arriving in Atlanta, Noel wasted no time in setting up practice and getting involved in city affairs. He may have seen in the frontier town of Atlanta, a burgeoning city, as it was fast becoming a major place of commerce.   Formerly known as "Terminus" in the 1830's, because of all the railroad lines flowing in and out, Atlanta was becoming the pride of the South. After Terminus it was called Marthasville after the Governor's daughter. A chief engineer working for the Georgia railroad company is credited for suggesting the name of Atlanta in 1845. Atlanta would claim the name of "Gate City".

The first known utterance of the term came during a toast in 1857 in Charleston, South Carolina. The Atlanta Mayor at the time was Judge Ezzard, who was in Charleston for a ceremony of the completed railroad from Charleston to Memphis. It was the first to connect the Atlantic Ocean and the Mississippi River.[1] They were toasting the various cities along the route. The toast to Atlanta went something like this, "The Gate City, the only tribute which she requires of those who pass through her boundaries is that they stop long enough to partake of the hospitality of her citizens." He coined the name as such because those travelling the route must pass through the Atlanta "gate". [2]

---

[1] Memphis and Charleston Railroad:
https://en.wikipedia.org/wiki/Memphis_and_Charleston_Railroad
[2] Franklin Garrett, "Atlanta & Environs" Vol 1. P432

At once, Dr. D'Alvigny entrenched himself in the medical community. A leader at heart, robust and eccentric, but was no doubt full of advice for the younger burgeoning doctors because he had been a long-time surgeon in France. The first presence of D'Alvigny was noted at a burial of a fellow doctor, James Nissen, who died while passing through Atlanta in 1850. He was the very first burial at the new "City Cemetery", now "Oakland Cemetery" on the east side of Atlanta. A small crowd gathered as Dr. D'Alvigny stood over the grave, and pulled out a knife. Swiftly, he plunged it into the neck of the corpse, and the crowd assuredly gasped! Dr. Nissen had a common fear of the times – being buried alive. Therefore, Dr. D'Alvigny was only performing his duties as his colleague had requested, by cutting his jugular vein.[3]

Around the time the D'Alvigny family arrived in Atlanta, there were eight to nine doctors residing in the city with the following population of approximately "400 heads of households, around 2,000 whites, 18 free negroes and about 500 slaves."[4] The famous, Dr. Crawford Long, originally of Jefferson, moved to Atlanta around this time. Dr. Long is noted as the first physician to successfully use anesthesia during surgery, a major milestone in medicine at the time. He brought his family, including five children, to live in Atlanta in 1850. One year later, however, he uprooted the family again and moved to Athens, Georgia, disliking the culture of the city.[5] The family had moved from a rural area. Perhaps the Longs were unhappy in a city environment, and thought it better to raise their children elsewhere, near family and friends. However, Dr. Long's legacy lived on in Atlanta with a hospital named for him in the 20th century. He had become famous for using sulfuric ether for anesthesia.[6]

---

[3] "First Oakland Burial in 1850", The Atlanta Georgian Feb 23, 1937 from Atlanta History Center

[4] Franklin Garrett, Ibid. (per Nov 1850 census)

[5] Garrett, Ibid. p

[6] Crawford Long on Wikipedia https://en.wikipedia.org/wiki/Crawford_Long

Pauline D'Alvigny Campbell – Civil War Nurse

The D'Alvigny's lived in a several places in Atlanta during the upbringing of Pauline and Charles. Initially, he had an office and residence in 1850 across from the Atlanta Steam Flouring Mill.[7] During these times a separate office was not affordable and it was not unusual practice to do so. Growing up in a doctor's house might seem unusual to us, but it was probably par for the course for wife and children. In no time at all, however, Pauline would begin her teenage years and start attending the balls and receiving gentlemen callers, no doubt.

The flouring mill was the first mill of its kind in Atlanta in the early part of the decade. Its founder, Richard Peters, was originally from Philadelphia, Pennsylvania. His ancestor was a Judge and associate of President George Washington. The story goes that he travelled by paddlewheel in the chilling cold winter of 1835 arriving first in Charleston, South Carolina and then making his way to Augusta where he was the chief engineer of the Georgia Railroad. It took eight years to construct the line from Augusta to Atlanta, which was then called Marthasville. People complained of the city name taken from the Governor's daughter, as it was too long to record in the railroad log books. Thus, Peters was partly responsible for the name being changed as he traded letters with the engineer who pinned the name, and started printing circulars with the new name of Atlanta. Due to lack of water in the immediate area, Peters had to power the mill by wood, thus purchasing several pine lots and operations near the railroad.[8] Today, this area is located at the site of the "Twin Towers" of Atlanta, the "Sloppy Floyd" government buildings. The mill was closed in the late 1850's and was purchased and converted to a pistol-making factory, which supplied arms during the Civil War. It was also one of the many buildings,

---

[7] The Atlanta Weekly Intelligencer newspaper (Atlanta, GA) 184-1855 March 22, 1855, Image 4 at gahistorcnewspapers.galileo.wg.edu

[8] Richard Peters on Wikipedia: https://en.wikipedia.org/wiki/Richard_Peters_(Atlanta)

slated for destruction by the Union army late in the War and burned to the ground.[9]

Pauline and Charles were still young children, when the following event happened in December of 1851, a time during the Holidays, when goodwill to all men should abide. There were two families whose lives became entwined when a local dentist, Dr. Hilburn married Martha Byrd, the daughter of John Byrd and his wife. There was trouble between Dr. Hilburn and the in-laws that had been escalating for some time. John Byrd had deeded a house in the city to his beloved daughter Martha, where she and her husband and children resided. The Byrds lived south of the city in a large Ante-bellum plantation.

One day they stopped their carriage in front of the piazza of the Hilburn family home, and in it sat Mrs. Byrd for hours, waiting for her husband. No one knows exactly why, but this occurrence did not set well with Dr. Hilburn, who proceeded to approach the buggy with a hatchet in hand. His intent was to destroy the carriage, as he started whacking at the top. Mrs. Byrd, incensed, managed to get the hatchet away from him, grab a stick or cane and start beating him. Elijah, Martha's brother, and also a carriage-maker by trade, saw his mother in distress. He pulled a short knife and stabbed Dr. Hilburn in the neck. Dr. D'Alvigny was summoned to the scene but could not make it in time, and Dr. Hilburn died within 5 minutes. Elijah Byrd was charged with murder. There was a trial and the jury sentenced him to death by hanging in 1853. With his father's help, it was appealed to the Supreme Court, the decision reversed, and eventually he was pardoned for the murder.[10] Perhaps this is one reason that Dr. Long felt Atlanta was a poor choice to raise a family.

---

[9] Stephen Davis 'What the Yankees Did to Us", (Mercer University Press 2012) p 10 & p370

[10] Franklin M. Garrett, "Atlanta and its Environs, A Chronicle of Its People and Events", (Lewis Historical Publishing Company Inc. 1954) Section VI "The Eighteen Fifties: Chapter 29: 1851: Volume 1 p 336-338.

Clarke: 1984 – Atlanta: Pounding the Pavement

I grew up in Atlanta, and went there looking for a job after college. If you ask a young person today, what does the phrase "pounding the pavement" mean? They may know, but have not literally experienced it. Today job-hunting is quite a different process than the 1980's. We have email, internet, I-phones and other technologies, but after my college graduation, for me, it meant, dressing up in a nice suit, with briefcase by my side. I would park in a central location in Atlanta, and walk on foot, in heels, in the heat of the Summer, heading to a test, interview or just stopping in somewhere along the way to hand-off my "paper" resume. This was a time when not everyone had a PC or laptop at home.

On one occasion I entered the looming "Twin Towers" in Atlanta to apply for a job with the state government. Lo and behold, when I walked through the door, there was one of my study-pals from West Georgia College in Carrollton, Georgia. We were both there for the same reason, although with different professional ambitions. His aim was for the Accounting Department, and mine for computer programming. It turns out that I didn't get the job, so there was more "pounding" for me.

In the same area is the sprawling campus of Georgia State University. One of the lots where Dr. D'Alvigny once lived and had his medical practice, is now one of the college buildings where classes are held. Dr. D'Alvigny would become part of a major building project in 1854, the first medical college in Atlanta. [11] It seems apropos that the doctor's old residence is now a University Science center, a ten story glass building, completed in 2010. [12] Rick attended GSU and I had one class

---

[11] Emory University School of Medicine History;
http://www.med.emory.edu/about/history/index.html-
[12] https://www.atlantadowntown.com/go/petit-science-teaching-and-research-laboratory-development The Parker H. Petit Science Center is part of the Georgia

there briefly, many years before Rick and I ever met. My mother and I went to classes one summer. It was a great time and memory. I recall meeting her at the Student Center for lunch, walking across Gilmer Street around Courtland Avenue. She had gone back to school after twenty years to pursue her passions, Art and Psychology.

Eventually, I did find work and by the end of the decade ended up going "West", such as now is the slogan of my alma mater. This time it was to Northwest Atlanta near Bolton, DeFoors Ferry and Howell Mill Roads. It turns out that the D'Alvigny family also moved about five miles to the west of Atlanta, to a town called Bolton, off DeFoors Ferry Road, in what is known today as Buckhead, a suburb of Atlanta.

Rick's father Tom grew up in the Buckhead area of town. Mayor Sam Massell, head of the Buckhead Coalition was interviewed and told the story of how the town, formerly Irbyville, got the name it has today. A hunter killed a deer, and displayed it in front of the Irby family store. Some say it was Henry Irby, the patriarch of the family, who owned a lot of land in the area who killed the deer. Around the year of 1838, people would say "Let's go meet at the Buck Head".[13] Rick's grandmother Mildred lived in the area near Lenox Square until the mid-1990's.

D'Alvigny: Mid-1850's
Atlanta Medical College

In early 1855 the Dalvigny's moved to Marietta Street where Dr. N. D'Alvigny states in his advertisement that "Patients

---

State University campus. On Lot 46 at the corner of Gilmer Street and Jessie Hill Jr today (formerly SW corner Decatur and Butler streets Lot 46, respectively , per 1853 Map per Franklin Garrett Atlanta Environs Vol 1 p 354) and Dr. D'Alvigny's advertisement in Atlanta Constitution.

[13] https://www.wabe.org/how-buckhead-got-its-name/ Interview with Sam Massell

for Surgical operations can be accommodated with board" and "Ladies wishing dental attendance, by giving a timely notice, even through the Post Office, will be furnished with a conveyance free of charge". [14] He was giving the ladies free transportation to his new home office, a little farther out than where he had lived.

While in Atlanta, Dr. D'Alvigny befriended the Westmoreland brothers, John and Willis who were co-founders of the Atlanta Medical College, which would many years later become Emory School of Medicine. In 1855 the college was built at the Northwest corner of Butler and Jenkins Streets in Atlanta, in a two story brick building with a cupola atop. Living just down the street while the college was under construction, Dr. D'Alvigny was involved from the beginning, and named Curator of the college. He had established quite a collection of instruments and medical materials by the time of the Civil War. He was especially close to Dr. Willis Westmoreland, who was Chief of Surgery at the college. Notably there was a mutual respect between the two surgeons. Two years before the hospital was chartered, Dr. Westmoreland went to Paris to attend several surgical lectures. [15] Back in Atlanta, Noel assisted Willis, who became the Head of Surgery at the college, as Prosector. (A prosector was a "person with the special task of preparing a dissection for demonstration, usually in medical schools or hospitals.") [16]. As a learning institution, unfortunately cadavers were often used, as well as deceased animals. One account mentions that Willis was thrilled with an experiment he was testing on a dog regarding some type of anesthesia. D'Alvigny being present at the time, viewed the excitement on the part of Willis as puzzling, and then turned to Willis in his

---

[14] Advertisement in Atlanta paper

[15] Find-a-grave https://www.findagrave.com/memorial/49467890/willis-foreman-westmoreland

[16] https://en.wikipedia.org/wiki/Prosector Definition of Prosector

thick French accent and exclaimed, "But Willis, the dog is Dead"![17]

Even with a medical college, Atlanta was still a young city, and lacking in many of the conveniences already occurring in much older areas. For instance, the city of Augusta Georgia already had gas street lamps, while Atlanta was still dim, dark and dangerous at night. Mr. Helme, founder of Atlanta Gas Light realized this and took action. He made a proposal to the city, to establish the coal-gas company, put up 50 gas street lamps for the city, and subsequently start supplying gas to the community.

They decided to light the first City lamppost on December 25th, 1855 to commemorate the occasion.[18] Before the ceremony began, a local resident, John Tomlinson, writes an advertisement in the paper, "we have just received from the North, a large number of gas pipes and fittings, with a full set of tools necessary to fit up Churches, Dwellings, Hotels, Stores and all other buildings in which Gas may be desired...ready to supply the citizens with Gas on Christmas Eve". He would have "satisfactory workers" and would be inspected by Mr. Helmes, the contractor.[19] How excited Mr. Tomlinson must have been of this good fortune, because several years ago in 1851, he was involved in a terrible accident, whereas a lumber train on the Macon and Western railway de-railed, and crushed his left arm. It was Dr. D'Alvigny who performed the amputation.[20] One of these lampposts would become so famous it is still talked about today. That story will be told later on in this book.

---

[17] Raffalovich, George, A Reed..ibid p 9

[18] James H. Pate, "Keeper of the Flame, the Story of Atlanta Gas Light Company 1856-1985"

[19] Pate, Ibid.

[20] Daily Constitutinalist, Augusta, Georgia 1846-1851, June 6, 1851 Image 2; from Atlanta Republican 4th inst. Gahistoricnewspapers.galileo.usg.edu.

CAMPBELL: Late 1850's Bolton near Peach Tree Creek

Up the road to the west of Atlanta in a town called Bolton, near Peachtree Creek, lived the Campbell family. The patriarch was Elias Campbell who owned a vast amount of land near Peachtree Creek off of DeFoors Ferry Road, and the Campbell's became prosperous farmers. One day in October 1855, standing in front of the Justice of the Peace, at just barely the age of seventeen years, Pauline Caroline D'Alvigny and Robert Campbell, one of Elias's sons, were joined together in marriage. Two years later, Pauline and Robert started a family with the birth of their first child, Evalina, followed by Helen in 1859. Then a baby boy would be born around two years later.[21]

Neighbor to the Campbells and D'Alvignys were the Huff's, husband Jeremiah and wife Elizabeth who lived on Huff Road, near Marietta Street with several children. The Huff house was built by Jeremiah Huff in the year before Robert and Pauline were wed. Among the Huff's children, were Sarah Huff, who was born in the house in 1856, and her older brother James, who would fight in the upcoming War. Pauline and Elizabeth became close friends.

Also not far from their farm was Judge Clark Howell, who owned a couple of mills including, Howell's Mill, a grist (grain) and sawmill for cutting lumber off of Peachtree Creek. He also became a judge in Fulton County in 1854.[22] In the early 1850's, Clark Howell, rented the home of Crawford Long in Atlanta, who had moved away. He later became Postmaster. People of the day heavily relied upon letters and newspapers to bring them news locally and nationally.

---

[21] Per 1860 Census records at ancestry.com- Boy's name believed to be Robert C. per later census records.
[22] Franklin Garrett, "Atlanta & Environs" Vol 1. 345,368

As the year of 1859 came to a close, the talk of the town would be surrounding the Raid at Harpers Ferry, part of Virginia which is today in West Virginia. On October 16, 1859, a violent revolt took place, led by the abolitionist John Brown. It was one catalyst to the War which was to come.[23]

In the early 1850's a historical-fiction book was written about slaves in plantations of the South who rose up against their owners. "Uncle Tom's Cabin" by Harriet Beecher Stowe of Connecticut quickly became a global best-selling novel.[24] From the South's viewpoint it was giving them a bad reputation, and making it appear that the cruelty and mistreatment of slaves was the norm and widespread in the Southern states. The book is said to have inspired a fellow Abolitionist, who was also in Connecticut, John Brown, to take action that would ultimately end his own life.[25]

Nine years after the book was published, at Harper's Ferry, Commonwealth of Virginia in 1859, John Brown, along with 21 men, seized the armory. He freed slaves and captured around 60 of the town's citizens, and a fight broke out. Many were killed in the incident, including the Mayor of the town. John Brown was hoping the freed slaves would rise up and join him in the insurrection. However, not one of the slaves participated in the uprising. Federal Colonel Robert E. Lee was sent with his troops to arrest Brown and his followers. Brown refused to surrender and was captured. There was a trial, and he was found guilty of treason and murder among other charges.[26] Most in the Northern states condemned his actions although some extremists saw him as a martyr. Nevertheless,

---

[23] Susan Pendleton Lee "New School History of the United States" (Richmond B.F. Johnson Publishing Co.1900)249

[24] Susan Pendleton Lee Ibid.p248-249

[25] Susan Pendleton Lee Ibid. p 248

[26] Susan Pendleton Lee, Ibid. p250

the event caused tensions between the North and South to fester even further.

Clarke: 2011 Harpers Ferry Landing – Rivers and Raids

On the one hundred and fiftieth anniversary of the first major Battle of the Civil War, Bull Run, Rick and I took a trip and visited the Harpers Ferry National Historic Park. We saw the displays within the red brick historical buildings near the peaceful flowing Shenandoah River by the railroad tracks, near the Potomac River, a meeting place for the two rivers. It was a beautiful area in the foothills of the Appalachian mountain range. We stopped by a large granite marker that read as follows, "On the night of October 16, 1859, Heywood Shepherd, an industrious and well respected colored freeman, was mortally wounded by John Brown's Raiders. In pursuance of his duties as an employee of the Baltimore & Ohio Railroad, he became the first victim of this attempted insurrection". The memorial was erected by the "United Daughters of the Confederacy" and the "Sons of the Confederate Veterans" as a memorial to Heyward Shepherd.[27] After the shock wore off, I pondered the irony. Three years after John Browns Raid, Harpers Ferry would see another battle on a much larger scale- Civil War.

---

[27] Harper's Ferry National Park - Monument to Heyward Shepherd by the United Daughters of the Confederacy and Sons of Confederate Veterans

Photo by Julie Clarke at Harpers Ferry National Park, WV

Atlanta Medical College [28]

[28] Barnard, George N, photographer. *Atlanta, before being burnt: by order of Gen'l. Sherman, from the cupola of the Female Seminary*. Atlanta Georgia United States, 1864. October. Photograph. https://www.loc.gov/item/2007662840/. Upper left hand corner of photo

Pauline D'Alvigny Campbell – Civil War Nurse

Chapter 3: 1860-61: War is Not for the Faint of Heart

"And lest your heart faint, and ye fear for the rumour that shall be heard in the land; a rumour shall both come one year, and after that in another year shall come a rumour, and violence in the land, ruler against ruler." Jeremiah 51:46 (KJV)

<u>WAR: South vs North:</u>
<u>Secession, Soldiers and Sunburn</u>

To consider how people felt at the time, I have included information from a Richmond Virginia history book published in 1900. This was the history book Rick's grandmother and great aunt used in school.[1]

In November 1860, Abraham Lincoln was elected President of the United States. Thus, many of the Southern states considering secession took action. The South did not desire war, but were taking their right to secede, which they had believed existed when the Constitution was drawn, described as the joining of independent states. [2] One of the major issues of secession involved the rights of the New Territories out west, such as Missouri, to make their own decision about slavery, as slavery was at that time allowed by the Constitution. Most of the Northern states, and Lincoln of the Republican Party, believed

---

[1] Susan Pendleton Lee is the author of the school history book. Her father William Nelson Pendleton was a teacher, preacher and soldier during the War. He was chief artillery officer under Robert E. Lee, and is known for naming his four cannons, Matthew Mark Luke & John. https://en.wikipedia.org/wiki/William_N._Pendleton; Susan married a second cousin of Robert E. Lee, Edwin Gray Lee. https://www.findagrave.com/memorial/10671/edwin-gray-lee

[2] Susan Pendleton Lee, "Lee's New School History of the United States" (B F Johnson Publishing Co. Richmond, Virginia 1900 p 253

that the Union must be saved, and slavery abolished. Two years before his election Lincoln, stated, "A house divided against itself cannot stand; I believe this government cannot endure permanently half slave and half free".[3] His main goal that he considered his duty as President was in keeping the Union together. Lincoln's mindset was against the recent Supreme Court decision (Dredd Scott in 1857) regarding expansion of slavery. This decision enforced Constitutional law ruling that slaves could be transferred with the family, and therefore the slave named Dred Scott was taken to Missouri and remained a slave in the New Territories. The South saw the decision as a victory and confirmation of their way of life. Even further, the South and North were divided. [4]

Things had been brewing between the North and South for some time, and South Carolina was the first to make the decision to secede. From the Southern perspective, the purpose of secession was not to extend nor preserve slavery, rather protect the states' rights to choose. While the right to own slaves is evident in the Confederate Constitution, it is not well known today that this new government's constitution "expressly prohibited African slave trade".[5] The Confederacy did not sanction bringing any more African slaves into the states from overseas. As is well known, all of the Southern states practiced slavery, while most of the Northern states did not own slaves with the exception of Delaware and Maryland, which had small percentages, 3% of households owned slaves, and 12% respectively. The Top three slave-holding states by the same standards were Mississippi, South Carolina and Georgia. Mississippi and South Carolina had more slaves than free persons. There were 37% of Georgia families who owned slaves,

---

[3] Abraham Lincoln, "Abraham Lincoln His Speeches and Writings', edited by Roy P. Basler, (Cambridge, MA Da Capo Press 2nd Edition) 2001 p 392
[4] Lee, Ibid 247-248
[5] Lee, Ibid. p 262-263

so the vast majority of Georgians did not.[6] It is believed that since this was not a compelling issue to them that most primarily fought not for slavery, but for their homes, state and honor.

Clarke: 2018 – The Bible Museum Washington DC

On our last day of vacation in Washington DC, we visited the new Bible Museum, which was quite impressive. I loved the second floor best – the Bible and Culture. I saw the display of Billy Graham, The C.S. Lewis book, the Chronicles of Narnia, and even Elvis's Bible. Then I turned the corner to view the displays of the Bible and the Civil War. The Bible played a role in defending the decisions of both sides. The museum showed both pro and anti-slavery arguments by various people of the 1850's and 60's, including Harriet Beecher Stowe and some Southern ministers. The North used passages from Deuteronomy to defend against slavery, which argued against "man-stealing" and principles of justice and equality, while the south contended that slavery itself was not admonished in the Bible.[7] Along with the Bible, each side also used the Constitution for their defense and both thought of themselves as patriotic.

---

[6] The 1860 Census results as mentioned the Civil War Home Page – www.civil-war.net *1997-2018*

[7] Museum of the Bible displays including Cotton is King, and Pro-Slavery Arguments by E.N. Elliott and statements of Harriett Beecher Stowe. (from visit to museum May 2018)

<u>WAR: 1861 Matters of</u>
<u>Secession and Aggression</u>

In January 1861, Georgia legislators made a declaration and voted to secede from the Union, and join the Confederate States of America. Many southerners at the time referred to the War as one of "Northern Aggression", and felt they had the Constitutional right to secede, and that the War was caused by the Northern attempt to preserve the Union.[8] In those times many citizens had more of an allegiance to the State where they resided than the Federal government. That is thought to be the main reason why Robert E. Lee turned down the offer from Lincoln to head-up the Federal Army, but instead he chose to stick by his "beloved Virginia". He would become the leader for the Southern Cause, and eventually the Commanding General under Confederate President Jefferson Davis.

A delegation was sent to Washington to request that the forts of South Carolina, including Fort Sumter be evacuated. One of the Judges assured this would be the case. Hearing of this the Southern military requested its surrender. They did not comply, so on April 12th 1861, shots were fired from the Battery in Charleston upon Fort Sumter. The fort was seized by Confederates. There were no casualties. The North claims it was South Carolina that started it, while South Carolina claimed the North started the War because they would not surrender.[9]

Lincoln was sworn in as President after some of the states seceded, and Senator Jefferson Davis became the President of the Confederate States of America. Between the 1860 succession of South Carolina and several other states, and the

---

[8] Susan Pendleton Lee ,Ibid. p253. P263
[9] Susan Pendleton Lee, Ibid. p257

end of the war in 1865, Abraham Lincoln was never officially the President of states such as South Carolina and Georgia.[10]

Clarke: 1998: Charleston Shrimp and Grits

The Ashley and the Cooper Rivers meet at the Atlantic ocean, on the East side of Charleston. Rick and I gazed out from the Battery on a blustery day, typical of a Charleston afternoon in the summer. There in the distance we could see the remnant of "Fort Sumter".

We took a ferry to see the remnants of the fort. Not much was left, but it left us with an experience of having been to a place with such history. Later we ate at one of the restaurants in town, across from where the "slave market" used to be. This area is now very touristy with an open-air buildings, mini-malls and kiosks near the river. On the menu was a local menu item, a tasty dish of scrumptious shrimp bites in a plethora of cheesy grits, simply called "Shrimp and Grits". This was also the names of the two horses who pulled us along on the carriage tour of the City as dusk was falling upon the narrow cobblestone streets. We lazily sauntered past many Charleston residences with their glorious iron gates , including the famous Rainbow Row, of the multi-colored homes, heading South toward the Battery, and up along the Antique district, near where the D'Alvigny's had lived many years ago.

During one of our stays, we got up early and had a delicious breakfast, with grits, of course, at our historic hotel. We arose early to take a Civil War tour, and the day wasn't too hot yet, or so I thought, but it was hot enough. Instead of taking a carriage tour we decided to do the Civil War walking tour.

---

[10] America's Story from America's Library, http://www.americaslibrary.gov/jb/civil/jb_civil_davis_1.html ; also brought up as a fact in Civil War Tour in Abbeville, SC

We began by standing right outside the hotel listening to the tour guide, and listening and listening. This wasn't much of a walking tour, I thought. My mind drifted, and I gazed up at the bright sun – and then down I went. I had fainted. Whisked to the hotel room, I was able to get some rest and re-bounded. The Civil War is not for the faint of heart.

D'Alvigny: 1860's Atlanta: On the Homefront

By the 1860's the Atlanta Medical college was deemed a success with a very capable faculty and "respectable museum", the latter being likely due to D'Alvigny who was the curator.[11] In 1861, after the War began, the board of the college voted to close its operations and it was determined that the building be used as a Confederate hospital. D'Alvigny was quick to offer his family, non-gratis, as volunteer nurses.[12] There were thousands of women in the South who volunteered to help the Cause of the South in some way. In Atlanta, the Ladies Relief Society sprang up that was headed by Maria Westmoreland, wife of Dr. Willis Westmoreland. Pauline was active in this society in addition to helping out her father with the wounded.[13] According to Mary Gay, a young single woman who lived in Decatur with her Mother, there was "patriotic co-operation" between women of Decatur and Atlanta in supplying aide such as knitting socks, supplying food and writing letters to "our soldiers".[14] Miss Gay had a half-brother named Thomas "Thomie" Stokes who signed

---

[11] Raffalovich, Ibid. p4 and ; https://newspaperarchive.com/atlanta-daily-southern-opinion-may-26-1868-p-1/

[12] Letter in the "Southern Confederacy" of August 2, 1861, by D'Alvigny, M.D. fn July 26 1861 to the Atlanta City Council

[13] Wendy Hammand Venet, "A Changing Wind, Commerce and Conflict in Civil War Atlanta", (New Haven, CT Yale University Press, 2014). p215

[14] "Life in Dixie During the War", by Mary A.H. Gay, Edited by J.H. Segars, 1861-1865, Mercer University Press 2001 edition. P42.

up in the 10th Regiment Texas infantry and served under General Joe Johnston in the Western theater.[15]

As for Georgian men, there was also the Confederate volunteer service for those who had not or couldn't sign up for duty. Pauline's brother Charles was seventeen years old when the War began. He was assigned to help out his father, Dr. D'Alvigny, who was in charge of the African Church hospital during the spring of 1861.[16]

The first major battle of the War was fought at Manassas, VA (aka Bull Run), in July 1861[17]. It was a Confederate victory.

CLARKE: 2011 – Manassas (Bull Run) Virginia-Battles and Buses

Rick and I arrived by train at the "un-manned" station at 8am on a Thursday morning and saw a well-dressed man standing there outside the station. He had some official looking pins on his shirt. Not many people had disembarked from the Amtrak Crescent train, and the few that did, dispersed quickly. As he approached us with a smile and outstretched hand, we asked him if he knew where our hotel was. We already knew it was walking distance of the station. He began telling us he was from New Jersey, and he knew the DC area very well. We were a bit confused, as we were in Manassas, Virginia! Then he walked off, so we just picked a direction to go, looking for Main Street. Shortly thereafter we saw the same man standing on a deserted street corner (except for us), and he was belting out "My Country Tis of Thee" and waving his arms. We headed in the opposite direction. Eventually, we did

---

[15] Thomie Stokes Gravesite Information. Find-a-Grave: https://www.findagrave.com/memorial/6550062/thomas-jefferson-stokes
[16] "Confederate Military History", Vol. 3 p 593
[17] Confederate forces typically named battles for the cities, and the Union used the names of the nearby creeks and waterways.

find the Inn. We had arrived at the start of festivities of the Sesquicentennial (150th) anniversary of the First Battle of Manassas (aka "Bull Run" to Yankees) the third weekend of July 2011. I was not much of a camper and glad we stayed in the hotel due to the heat.

When we visited the campsite to visit Rick's fellow re-enactors, it was like stepping into an oven. There was hardly any breeze or trees to shade the rows of tents. They were expecting 9,000 re-enactors to participate in the battle on Saturday. Rick had been battling a cold, and wasn't in tip-top shape to participate, but come Saturday, we awoke early to catch the shuttle bus to the Battle. After arriving at the parking lot, Rick realized he had forgotten his canteen. We weren't sure if he would have a chance to buy one from the sutlers (period vendors), so I went back to the hotel to retrieve it . As we boarded the bus we discovered the event organizers wanted to make sure everyone, both soldiers and civilians were well hydrated, so they gave each person at least two bottles of water. We could use it. That day it was 105 degrees but it felt even hotter. There were 11,000 spectators at the event, many which had to stand behind the cannons which were named Matthew Mark Luke & John by the re-enactors. It was Reverend William Nelson Pendleton in charge of artillery that named them after the four books of the Gospel. Back in 1861 it was only 80-something degrees, and there were civilian spectators then who came from Washington DC and brought a picnic to view the battle. They soon realized the horrors of war and became in danger themselves, fleeing the scene in their buggies.[18]

The Battle was from 9:30am to noon. I wasn't able to see Rick anywhere, even with his new Havelock-Kepi hat that resembled the French Foreign legion attire, which covered the ears. The battle took place early in the War when companies

---

[18] Curt Johnson and Mark McLaughlin, "Battles of the Civil War", 1977 Roxby Press; 1995 Barnes & Noble 40; https://en.wikipedia.org/wiki/William_N._Pendleton

and units of both sides picked their own uniforms and chose any color, such as blue, grey, red and even green outfits. Also, some units were carrying their state flag. This complicated things, as soldiers sometimes couldn't determine "the enemy" and would fire on their fellow comrades (aka friendly fire). Later on in the War, there was more of the traditional blue for North and Grey for South. This was the battle where General Thomas "Stonewall" Jackson got his nickname, for having stood firm like a "stone wall" alongside his troops. A Colonel at the time, there is a story that Jackson was lining up his men, unsure, anxious, getting ready for battle on the field. A Confederate General Bee asked who that was standing there "like a stone wall"?[19]

As I tried to find Rick among the crowds after the battle was over, little did I know that for us, the battle was not quite over yet – even when Taps was played and the re-enactors were leaving the field. Rick called me on the cell phone (yes, they are allowed) after the Battle and, I met him with plenty of water and some Gatorade in hand. After some rest, but not nearly enough, we started to the bus, which was a bit of a hike. Rick started to feel ill when we saw the long lines to board. We made it to a tent near the bus stop. Rick was feeling queasy and decided to lie down and nearly fainted, so a Gator vehicle took us back, (from where we started) to the medical tent for him to get cooled off. They assured me they could give us a ride back to the buses. (Not true). After a long time of rest we knew it was getting late, but couldn't find a ride. I suggested that Rick eat a hamburger, and I headed toward the Information booth to find us some transportation. The booth was empty, and then we heard on the loud speaker the event is closing and the last bus leaves at 3:15. I looked down at my watch: It was 3:00pm. We walked as fast as we were able, and got within 50 feet or so, and I saw the last bus pulling away in front of us. Like a mad woman I started yelling "Stop!!" and waving my arms. The bus paused and opened the door.   Praise God!

---

[19] Johnson & McLaughlin, Ibid. p.39

We were exhausted when we finally got to the hotel, and we both crashed. But, we had paid a pretty price for those tickets to the ball – which was Saturday evening at an "outdoor" pavilion, within walking distance from the Inn. I was determined to go. Rick also said he felt like going, so we got ready and went. I was thinking it might cool off when the sun went down, but no such luck. On top of that, I had gotten sunburned earlier in spite of applying sunscreen twice. We both had sweat pouring from us, even as the evening wore on. I was too tired to even dance. Instead we ate, drank some sodas and just sat there talking to a lady at our table. In spite of our lackluster, we had a great time. We enjoyed hearing the black speaker talking about his heritage while waving the Confederate flag under which the speaker's black ancestor fought.[20] It was getting late, so Rick and I sauntered back towards the Inn under the moon. On the way back our favorite period band was playing on one of the side streets. We paused for a moment and let the music fill us. Tired, hot and dehydrated, but it was a time of celebration. We survived the Battle!

WAR: Continues in the East - Mississippi

The confederate forces were mounting, as many of the other states formed more regiments, and adopted the Confederate constitution. This included the state of Mississippi who had soldiers at First Manassas. The month after the first major battle of the War, in August of 1861, a soldier by the name of John H. Duke, at the age of around twenty years old, signed up under Captain E.R. Neilson with the 27th Mississippi Infantry called "Rayburns Rifles" Company D. He was from upper Northeast Mississippi, from Tallahatchie County. In the summer of 1860 he had lived with his parents David and Nancy Duke, being the oldest, having four brothers and three sisters.

---

[20] https://www.theroot.com/yes-there-were-black-confederates-here-s-why-1790858546 "The Root" online magazine article dated 1/20/2015, John Stauffer, "Yes there were Black Confederates and Here's Why"

The county they lived in was formerly under the Choctaw Indian nation, meaning "Rock of Waters". [21] Private Duke would first be sent to the south-most Florida and Alabama line, and ultimately end up in the Atlanta Campaign. Georgia would also be forming more regiments on infantry and artillery. There will be more information on John Duke to come and how he fits in with the story.

---

[21] History of Tallahatchie County, Mississippi:
https://en.wikipedia.org/wiki/Tallahatchie_County,_Mississippi

150th Anniversary Saturday Battle of Manassas/Bull Run[22]

[22] Confederates in foreground. The two Women in white at the lower left are field nurses (aka Angels of the Battlefield) 150th Manassas VA July 2011 Photos by Julie Clarke

Chapter 4: 1862 Leyden's Artillery 9TH Georgia Battalion

"And I looked, and, behold, a whirlwind came out of the north, a great cloud, and a fire infolding itself, and a brightness was about it, and out of the midst thereof as the colour of amber, out of the midst of the fire. Ezekiel 1:4 (KJV)

In August of 1862, Dr. John P. Logan was put in charge of all Atlanta hospitals, and Dr. Willis Westmoreland in charge of the Atlanta Medical college hospital.[1]

While many Georgians had already begun the fight for what Southerner's referred to as "The Cause", Pauline's family, specifically her husband, Robert, and her father Dr. D'Alvigny (who was sixty two years old), signed up in April 1862 with Leyden's Artillery, 9th Georgia Battalion Light Artillery, Company A[2]. In her very own words (indicated in bold throughout), this is Pauline's personal account of "The War".[3] The following starts the beginning of her story in the town of Bolton (in Buckhead today), as her husband leaves her in charge of their farm on Peachtree Creek.

PAULINE: "In the year 1862, my husband joined Leyden's battalion of artillery, leaving me at home with three small children and one negro to work for our support, but we had plenty to live upon."

LEYDEN'S ARTILLERY: Austin Leyden was a member of a Georgia Volunteer Infantry, formed before the War, called the "Gate City Guards". He was also a fellow mason and neighbor of

---

[1] Jack D. Welsh, "Two Confederate Hospitals and Their Patients, Atlanta to Opelika"(Macon, GA Mercer University Press 2005), p14
[2] Application for Pension by a Widow Under Act of 1910, State of Georgia Pauline submitted in July 1912, plus Fold3 compiled service records
[3] Atlanta Pioneer Women's Society Records, 1909-1984 and <u>Sarah Huff papers, 1862-1939.</u> James G. Kenan Research Center Manuscript CollectionsMSS 120

Dr. D'Alvigny.[4] His stately house on Peachtree Street was one of the most elegant Greek revival styled homes in Atlanta at the time. So well admired was his residence that Margaret Mitchell had the Butlers (Scarlet and Rhett) living next door to the Leyden's. (The columns are said to reside today at the Peachtree Apartments in the Ansley Mall area of Atlanta.)[5]

A pioneer of Atlanta, Major Leyden was founder of the Atlanta Machine Works, a company used by the Confederacy to produce war materials. He left the "Guard" in March of 1862 to form and lead the 9th Georgia Artillery Battalion in the War Between the States. Dr. D'Alvigny helped organize the Unit and enlisted in Company A, the first of 5 companies, A through E. Pauline's husband, Robert Campbell joined Leyden's light artillery Company A on May 7th, 1862, and was subsequently assigned to Company B as a Hospital cook. As Pauline's father was the official surgeon of Leyden's Artillery at its inception, it comes as no surprise that his son-in-law would be included in his staff of the field hospital.[6]

The month before Robert signed up, another major Battle of Shiloh in Tennessee had been fought and was a Union victory. This was credited to General Sherman, and shown as the first of his successful wages of War working alongside Grant.[7] This was even before Grant's ascension up the ranks under Lincoln. And it was the start of a beautiful friendship between the two Generals.

There was a soldier named James McMurtrey who enlisted in Company B of Leyden's artillery in March of 1862, at the age of twenty-four years. He left behind his wife, Lucinda with a small son, Willie in Sandy Springs, Georgia to tend the

---

[4] Franklin Garrett- Atlanta and Environs
[5] Peachtree Circle Apartments and Old Leyden House columns; ww.atlantapreservationcenter.com/place_detail?id=261&pt=1&year=all
[6] Joseph T. Derry; Edited by Clement Evans"Confederate Military History, v VI Atlanta Ga, Confederate Publishing Company, 1899, pp 142-143 Listing of officers
[7] John S.D. Eisenhour, "American General, The Life and Times of William Tecumsah Sherman" (Penguin Group New York)2014 p 102

farm.[8] McMurtrey wrote to his wife about the company's whereabouts and assignments. He became a teamster, which drove the horses or mules carrying wagons or other light artillery. Light artillery meant that speed was a factor, and another word commonly used was "horse artillery", as at one time 12 cannons were individually pulled by a 6 to 8 horse team.[9] In his letters he mentioned how well the camp was fed, most of the time. At one time he was sick and was sent to a nearby hospital 10 miles away, before returning to camp.[10] Though McMurtrey didn't mention Robert in his letters, I can imagine the two farmers discussing food, and their crops such as corn and wheat.

Private McMurtrey mentioned coming up through Dalton, Georgia on the way to the Battalion's first assignment in Abingdon Virginia. Around that time there was some unexpected activity brewing in the spring of 1862, including what is now known as the "Great Locomotive Chase" on April 12th.[11] A group of Union soldiers formed a spy ring, led by Kentuckian James Andrews, and called themselves Andrews Raiders, dressed in civilian clothes and boarded a train bound for Chattanooga. Captain William Allen Fuller, conductor of the Western & Atlanta railroad engine, the "General", pulled into Big Shanty (Kennesaw) and bellowed for everyone to disembark for breakfast at the Lacy Hotel, which was their usual custom. As he was partaking of the delicious food placed before him, he happened to notice his train pulling out of the station. Jumping to his feet, he took off like lightning on foot, after his engine followed by a single railcar. Anthony Murphy, a Western & Atlantic Railroad official, and the engineer Cain joined him in chasing down the stolen train. Using the help of several engines they took control of, the trio and eventually caught up with "The

---

[8] Mrs. J.H. Johnston, Letters to Lucinda 1862-1864; (located at Emory Archives) 1985 and Fold3
[9] Johnston, Lucinda letter, Ibid. Sept 1, 1862
[10] Mrs. J.H. Johnston, Letters, Ibid. Nov 12th, 1862 sick at Emory Henry Hospital
[11] Franklin Garrett, Environs Vol1 Chapter 40 Year of 1862 p520, 521

General" after a wild chase. Seven of the Raiders were caught and hung, including Andrews. Several were taken prisoner, later being swapped, and a few others escaped and made it up North.[12]

Back in another part of the Eastern Theater of Virginia, near the Confederate capital of Richmond, General Johnston was in charge of the Confederate Army and was combatting Union forces. Johnston was wounded during The Battle of Seven Pines on May 31st and June 1st of 1862. The Union General McClellan was gaining ground, so Jefferson replaced Johnston with General Robert E. Lee. Johnston was severely injured so, General Robert E. Lee would remain the Confederate Commander for the remainder of the War.[13]

Robert Campbell, with Company B was assigned under General Marshall's Army at Camp Cumming in Abingdon, VA, arriving on or before September 1st 1862. This was a strategic location because they were near the Salt mines in Tazewell County Virginia, and a lot of their time was spent defending the mines. A presence there was absolutely vital to the Confederacy. Lucinda mentioned the deficiency and need for salt, even asking her husband if he could possibly send her some, which he unfortunately was unable to do so.[14] Back in the 1860's salt was a necessary and valuable commodity used for food preservation. Salt also had other major war-related purposes. It was needed to produce the chemical, Saltpeter, used for gunpowder. [15] Times were hard on the home front during the War for the women and children.

The state of Kentucky was a divided state with some siding with the Union. Therefore the families of Confederate

---

[12] Franklin Garrett, Environs Ibid. p 523

[13] "Voices of the Civil War Atlanta, Fall of the South's Gate City, Time Life Books & Time Warner Audiobooks 1996

[14] Johnston, Letters, of Jan 23 1863 Ibid.

[15] Historic Crab Orchard Museum and Pioneer Park, Tazewell County, Virginia museum display photo from 2010

soldiers had been ordered to leave the state of Kentucky. The local Kentuckians, in the Mountains, had been persuaded and were now excited to fight with the Confederacy. Around 5000 Enfield rifles and muskets were ordered.[16] Remaining in the general vicinity, in November, per Captain Sentell's resignation letter, Leyden's battalion was stationed at Jeffersonville in November 1862.[17] The town of Jeffersonville is now called Tazewell Virginia.

Clarke: 2010: Tazewell County, Virginia

I simply love redbirds, known as Cardinals, and when we approached the Visitor center not far from Tazewell, Virginia, I saw the beautiful state bird on just about everything from the Welcome sign to the brochures. After getting our bearings straight, we proceeded to the town. Once we arrived, we saw a beautiful mural and confederate monument of a soldier in the town square. It was a quaint little town in the middle of forests and mountains. We found our way past homes and cows in pastures to the Historic Crab Orchard Museum, which had a lot of interesting artifacts. One display was about a female spy named Molly Tynes who would ride her horse to warn the town of Yankees coming.[18]

---

[16] Letters From Lucinda p 765

[17] Captain Sentell's resignation letter, Camp Lookout near Jeffersonville, VA – November 19, 1862
http://ancestrallychallenged.com/forum/index.php?showtopic=2295&st=0&

[18] Historic Crab Orchard Museum and Pioneer Park, Tazewell County, Museum display from Photo taken in 2010

Fall of 1862- The Wilderness Road

LEYDEN'S ARTILLERY: While Pauline was left home to oversee the farm and tend to their three small children, Robert, who has switched to Company B, was facing horrible conditions out in the elements of the Virginia Mountains, with rain, snow and freezing temperatures. James told Lucinda about his month long trip into the rugged mountains of Moccasin Gap. This is part of the famous route called the "Wilderness Road" that Daniel Boone cut through the mountains towards western Kentucky. The road was later known as the Mt. Sterling Pound Gap Road, originally an Indian trail, and was used in the 1800's to transport livestock back and forth. Also, salt from the mines of Saltville and iron from central Kentucky went into the state of Virginia on this road. McMurtrey called it the "worst road" travelling 4 miles upward with the ammunition and wagons on Guess Mountain, where they ran into the locals he described as "ignorant and barefooted people who didn't know what a negro was". Eventually they passed by the breastworks at Pound Gap[19]. There had only been minor skirmishes here – as it passed from Union hands into control of the Confederates in September of 1862.

Clarke: 2011: Sharpsburg (Antietam) The Sunken Road

On September 17, 1862, the second day at Sharpsburg (Antietam) Virginia a battle ensued that would be the bloodiest single day of the War. There were 12,400 Union and over 10,000 rebel soldiers killed, captured or wounded. There is a sunken road where much of the fighting took place, that's called

---

[19] Johnston, Letters, Ibid Dec 4 1862 letter to Lucinda

"Bloody Lane" due to the loss of life where Confederates and Yankees fought for 2 hours.[20]

Rick and I toured the battlefield by car with a CD guiding us. It became one of my favorite battlefields, as it did not cover a whole lot of space, and the different significant spots were laid out well. Generals McClellan and Lee were the two opposing commanders. There was not a real winner for this one, as Lee's loss in casualties was 1 out of 5 men, while the Union army ratio was 1 to 7 in casualties. We walked up a tower to see the view – basically a small farming community near the Antietam Creek, like a patchwork of cornfields, trees and farms. We saw the Dunker church that was used as a hospital. The famous nurse, Clara Barton, who founded the Red Cross attended the wounded for the Union side. Over 3600 died here.[21]

WAR: November 1862: King of Kentucky

LEYDEN'S ARTILLERY: As the soldiers were camping at the foot of the mountain, around 2am the unit was awakened by gun fire and ordered to "geer" up the horses, but it was a false alarm. In the month of October it was rainy and cold. Once they crossed Pounds Gap, the Eastern side of the Cumberland Gap region, McMurtrey mentions being at "rock house" near the hot springs which were covered boiling and bubbling up dark oil, even in the cold. One day they had 6 inches of snow. He mentions that a blind lady came to the camp to talk to the doctor, presumably D'Alvigny, as he was the company surgeon at the time. McMurtrey observed, "she listen(ed) to him with as much attention as if he had (been) a king".[22]

---

[20]William C. Davis, "Rebels & Yankees the Battlefields of the Civil War" Salamander Books, London, 2004 p 79, 81
[21] William C. Davis, Rebels Ibid.
[22] Johnston, Letters from Lucinda

Another story of McMurtrey was about Captain Peeples Division of the battalion. Peeples was over Leyden's company E, (Gwinnett Artillery). McMurtrey tells that one night, one of his comrades went to the nearby orchard to grab some apples, but never returned. It was thought the soldier deserted, which is punishable by hanging, but later on his wife was still writing to him, and he didn't show up at home. While the artillery unit was not in battle, there was still danger present in the area. There were Yankee snipers lurking around as one of the men on guard heard some rustling in the leaves, and saw several of them running off. The Confederates were able to capture one of their horses. The battalion later camped at a nearby steam mill. There were 3,000 Yankees a few miles away, but instead of a confrontation with them, Company B was ordered back to Jeffersonville, Tazewell County.[23]

In December of 1862, right before Christmas, Dr. D'Alvigny arrived at his home in Atlanta on furlough. He had written a letter to the commander of Cobb's Legion, where his son was serving, to have Charlie D'Alvigny assigned with him so they may have Christmas together. It was denied. After falling off a horse while marching back from Kentucky, Noel had been injured, and was home for a while. Meanwhile, Leyden's artillery, currently in Jeffersonville Virginia, was instructed on December 29th, to go "without delay", to Saltville and position themselves to defend the Salt-works. The enemy had been seen approaching the area, with as many as 4,000, and General Marshall was unaware of their immediate target.[24]

ORPHAN BRIGADE: Kentucky was a border state that was considered part of the Union forces, as it never seceded and was officially never in the Confederate States of America. The

---

[23] Johnston Letters, Ibid

[24] "The War of the Rebellion, the Compilation of the Official Records of the Union", Volume XX Chapter 32 December 31st 1862 p106

term you may have heard of frequently when speaking of the Civil War, "brother against brother", was an all too familiar phrase for Kentuckians, and hit close to home. You may recall James Andrews, the leader of the Raiders that stole the General. He was a Kentucky civilian who worked for the Union army, and is rumored that he played both sides. However, there were several Regiments from Kentucky that fought for the Confederacy, one which was called the "Orphan Brigade". It got its name after the 2nd Battle of Murfreesboro Tennessee when their commander, Breckinridge, ordered them to make a suicidal charge from a higher command. His brigade was slaughtered in the battle which began December 31st into January 1863. He rode through the woods, crying "My poor orphans!", so the name stuck years later.[25] In November of 1862, Private William H. Van Meter joined the brigade.[26] You will find out more about how Van Meter fits into Pauline's story later on. There is also another young soldier of pertinence who was mentioned earlier from 27th Mississippi by the name of Private John Duke.

WAR: The Battle of Pensacola

MISSISSIPPI 27: The first regimental assignment of the 27th Mississippi was in Mobile, Alabama in late 1861 into 1862, when they were sent a special assignment to Pensacola in February. They were to guard the Fort Barrancas and Fort McRee, and dismount all the heavy artillery there for shipment. They were stationed at the Naval yard which was overrun with fleas. Even so, they had plenty of good fish to eat. There was a proposal to the men while in Alabama to re-form and become the 1st Mississippi Artillery. Overwhelming they said "No" because in their minds, the War would soon be over and they would not be

---

[25] Orphan Brigade Nickname: https://en.wikipedia.org/wiki/Orphan_Brigade
[26] www.fold3.com; Compiled service record of William H. Van Meter

able to fight.[27] At this time they had no idea how long and hard their fate would be.

Clarke: 2012: The Blue Angels

My sister, who lived near Pensacola Beach, invited us to see the "Blue Angels" for the first time.[28] Sweat poured off our bodies, laying there on the beach in the heat of summer. Finally, there they were, showing off in the clear blue heavens. Known as the famous "Blue Angels" of the U.S. Navy, they really put on a show, making rings of smoke in the sky. They were sleek and fast. Then out of nowhere- they were only feet from us, gliding over the sands, you could even make out the face of the pilot swooshing above us, then up, back into the sky. What a sight to behold! I will never forget it. Next we went to the US Naval museum and saw all of the war planes. There was also a balloon displayed, so Rick and I climbed in and had our picture taken. It has been established that balloons were used on both sides of the Civil War for spying, but they were rarely successful and abandoned by the end of the War.[29] The wounded and weary soldiers of War were not abandoned by the dedication of nurses such as Clara Barton, the "blue angel" of the North and Pauline, the "gray angel" of the South.

---

[27]R.A. Jarman, I Full text "History of Company K, 27th Mississippi Infantry and is first and last muster rolls", Aberdeen Examiner, Aberdeen, MS 1890. P1-2

[28] Blue Angels aircraft are F/A-18 Hornet planes; https://en.wikipedia.org/wiki/Blue_Angels#Aircraft Blue Angles, Air Shows on Wikipedia

[29] Civil War Ballooning://www.battlefields.org/learn/articles/civil-war-ballooning "American Battlefield Trust"

CLARKE 2018: FORT BARRANCAS-The First Shot?

On my next trip to see the Blue Angels, in 2018, I visited Fort Barrancas at the NAS (Naval Air Station) in Pensacola. I had tried to visit it on a prior trip but we happened to just miss it, somehow, as it was closing when we got there. I had forgotten this, so after touring the museum, we headed over there – and again, it was closing up, 15 minutes earlier than the time stated. I ran over the dried up moat to the door of the fort, but it was shut tight. I then yelled to the ranger on the other side. He said it was closed but would be open tomorrow. So, I decided to come the next day stopping there on the way home back to Atlanta, skipping over the Visitor Center there and heading straight to the fort. A busload was leaving and I was there all by myself, going in and out of the tunnels, up and down dark stair passages, and then to the grassy top. There were some barrels of gunpowder on display, and a picture of the soldiers supplying the fort with arms in 1861. It took about an hour and I really wanted to see the gift shop. Went by there to get a brochure, and it was closed- Again! I had to leave, but at least I got to see the fort John Duke and his comrades defended and supplied with ammunitions. And perhaps I saw one of the Oak trees where they sat in its shade on a blustery day. It is also said that the first shot was fired here at Fort Barrancas in January 1861 when the Federals had charge of the fort and a drunken intruder was hanging around there – then a blank shot was fired. A Union soldier, claimed this after the war, saying the Union troops could claim they were there at the first shot of the Civil War.[30] This has been de-bunked as not being that significant, yet it is still recognized by some in Pensacola.

---

[30] "Melissa Nelson, Associated Press, "Back off SC, Fla Claims First Shot of the Civil War", 4/13/2011; http://www.nbcnews.com/id/42569813/ns/us_news-life/t/back-sc-fla-claims-first-shot-civil-war/#.W2YAjrgnaM8

CONFEDERATE READ ARTILLERY SHELL

3 inch cast iron shell made in Richmond, VA
Found in Saltville, Virginia

On loan from Scott Cole

The Historic Crab Orchard museum , Tazewell County Virginia 2012. On display was a Confederate Read Artillery Shell on loan from Scott Cole found in Saltville, Virginia

Sunken Road at Sharpsburg, Maryland, 2011

Fort Barrancas in 1861 – Photo taken from display in 2018"The Moat 1861: Confederates moving guns into Fort Barrancas"

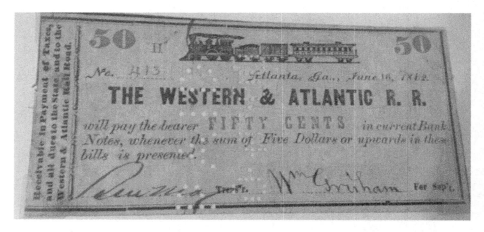

A 50 cent Change bill of the W&A Railroad of June 16, 1862

Chapter 5: 1863:
Trodden Down-hill With Horses

"Ye are the salt of the earth: but if the salt have lost his savour, wherewith shall it be salted? it is thenceforth good for nothing, but to be cast out, and to be trodden under foot of men. [14] Ye are the light of the world. A city that is set on an hill cannot be hid." Matthew 5:13-14 (KJV)

CLARKE: Trip to Lincoln's Cottage Washington DC, May 2018

The Amtrak train was two hours late when we arrived in Washington DC. We were heading over to see a Revolutionary battle and "meet" George Washington and the Marquis de Lafayette at Mount Vernon. We did not think we would make that, or even the Lincoln cottage that we wanted to see, but we had the best hotel concierge ever. She got us to both places during our stay. The cottage is Lincoln's get-away home that he stayed at in the summer of 1862 and 1863, which was at an Old Soldier's retirement home. During the war, he was often seen riding about, going back and forth by horse, from the White House. It was in the days before Camp David. We took a tour of the house, mostly void of furniture, but we did see a replica of the desk where they say Lincoln wrote much of the Emancipation Proclamation. Lincoln wrote the proclamation to state the secondary focus of the War which purported the freeing of slaves. It did not free every single slave in the U.S, but only those from states in rebellion against the Union. Not a law by Congress, rather an executive order, the document says that the U.S. will "recognize and maintain the freedom of such persons".[1] This was proclaimed under his authority as commander and chief of the military forces, on January 1st 1863,

---

[1]https://upload.wikimedia.org/wikipedia/commons/e/e4/Emancipation_Proclamation_WDL2714.jpg - Emancipation Proclamation on Wikimedia.org

after threatening the rebelling states in September 1862, that if they did not return to the Union, he would free their slaves. The slaves were officially emancipated by the passage of the Thirteenth amendment, near the close of the War.[2]

LEYDEN'S ARTILLERY: On February 1st, still entrenched in Saltville, Major Leyden was warned about a very large impending raid about to occur on the salt works by the enemy approaching from Kentucky. Leyden's battalion was to wait further instructions on where to position themselves. In this month, Private McMurtrey mentioned the harsh weather conditions they had endured, and that it had snowed a total of 21 days on and off through the winter. The company remained in the defense of the Salt works in the area, including around Bristol, Tennessee at Camp King, and then were ordered back to Moccasin Gap, Virginia, at the end of March 1863.[3] In the spring of 1863 the artillery stayed in the region of East Tennessee and Kentucky and its mission was to keep Union raiders at bay, as there were many Yankees in the region.[4]

On March 11, 1863, D'Alvigny wrote a letter from Atlanta, to the Secretary of War, resigning from duty, citing his advanced age, and the injury which caused his health to decline to the point that he could not continue as Surgeon of the 9th Georgia Battalion. D'Alvigny stated, "Please Believe Sir, that if my Capacities equaled my Patriotism nothing but the End of the War Would have induced me to quit the Command to which I was so glorious to Belong to."[5] However, D'Alvigny would continue to serve the cause as surgeon at the Atlanta Medical College hospital that Dr. Willis Westmoreland was currently

---

[2] Lee's New School book, Ibid. p 299

[3] Mrs. Johnston, MdMurtrey letters, Ibid. March 26 and 30th 1863 letters to Lucinda from McMurtrey

[4] Confederate Veteran Oct 1920 p 389

[5] Fold3.com Image printed May 25, 2014 Letter to James Seddon Secretary of War, written and signed by Noel D'Alvigny March 11, 1863.

under control of. He also had the help of his family and the
Ladies Society who was very helpful in supplying clothing for the
hospital patients in Atlanta. This was reported to Dr. Logan,
from the Doctor in charge of Gate City Hospital[6]

Although Dr. D'Alvigny is free from marching and risking
falling off another horse in the army, he is not free from being a
doctor. The war will soon come close to him. Lincoln talks
about freedom in his Emancipation Proclamation. Earlier that
year, the January 25, 1863 issue of *The Southern Confederacy,*
reported that even the in Northern states such as Indiana there
is no cheering the recent messages from Lincoln. The newspaper
quoted, "That in the President's late message we see nothing to
cheer the heart of the patriot, or that promises peace to the
country, and we do now declare that we have no confidence in
the patriotism of the President or his advisers, and that we
unqualifiedly condemn his policy of emancipation"[7]

The War for Southern Independence had a victory at
Chancellorsville but had one huge loss in leadership. The
Southern Confederacy newspaper reported as follows, "our
greatest loss was in the wounding of Gen. T. J. Jackson, who
suffered amputation of the arm at the shoulder-joint."[8] Lee lost
his right arm by losing Stonewall Jackson who died after the
amputation from pneumonia.[9] Stonewall would not be able to
help Lee at Gettysburg.

---

[6] Stout Papers, March 23, 1863 letter from Dr. Paul Eve, surgeon at Gate City
Hospital). From Emory Archives- Stuart A. Rose Manuscript, Archives, and Rare Book
Library; Stout, Samuel Hollingsworth 1822-1903 papers

[7] "Strong Resolutions passed by the Democracy of Huntington County Indiana",
Southern Confederacy, January 25,1863 1

[8] "Special Correspondences of the Constitutionalist History of the Late Great Battles
in Virginia Headquarters Wright's Brigade in the Field Near Fredericksburg, May
5th,1863" *Southern Confederacy,* May 13, 1863

[9] This Day in History: Thomas j. Stonewall Jackson dies" May 10, 1863.
https://www.history.com/this-day-in-history/thomas-j-stonewall-jackson-dies

CLARKE: 2012: GETTYSBURG Wenches, Ghost-hunting and the Underground

Pauline's brother Charles fought in Gettysburg in July 1863 under Cobb's Legion Calvary. Rick had several other Confederate ancestors who fought, so we took the trip in 2012. We stayed at an old historic hotel in the town and ate at a neat Tavern that was partially underground. Little light made the place very dark. The waitresses were dressed in period attire, such as Wenches in Medieval times. They told us that the place was on the "underground railroad", and the fireplace was used to secretly hide and transfer slaves during the Civil War. After seeing the awesome Battlefield during the day, we did a ghost tour at night. Did we see any Confederate soldiers? Well, the highlight was that we passed by an orphanage that was very eerily lit, and a creek where soldiers had died. I saw no ghosts, however.

ATLANTA: It was reported that among all Atlanta hospitals the Medical College was the cleanest hospital.[10] Soon there would be even more wounded to come. Per the Stout Papers, Dr. Logan wrote of the ten or so thousand men sent into Atlanta in the weeks following the Battle of Chickamauga (September 1863). Inadequate facilities of Atlanta hospitals only had room for 1800 total, and were thus overwhelmed. In October, an undisclosed correspondence commended the medical officers who worked tirelessly in their skilled craft and made order out of confusion.[11] While D'Alvigny was attending the wounded, on July 31st, 1863, Leyden's Artillery was stationed under Colonel

---

[10] Jack, D Welsh, Two Confederate Hospitals, Ibid. p17
[11] Stout papers per Emory archives Ibid.

Trigg (Robert) in the 2nd brigade, which was headquartered in Knoxville, TN[12]

ORPHAN BRIGADE: From May to October 1863, Private Van Meter was sick in several North Georgia hospitals including Rome.[13] William Van Meter had left his family in Bowling Green, Kentucky in the 1860's to fight for the Confederacy. While he was recuperating, his brigade was on the front lines at the Battle of Chickamauga, Georgia in September. After a six month long time of illness, Van Meter returned to service in November of 1863.

CLARKE: July 20, 2005: Mammoth Cave

This was our first visit to Kentucky. We went to "Mammoth Cave National Park" and took the "strenuous" Frozen Niagara tour. It started with a descent down 300 metal stairs at the entrance to the cave. I was at first dreading this because of my knee issues, but it ended up being a great cave experience, and one of the best I've ever seen. Rick and I then took a short cruise down the "Green River" and saw deer and turtles. We decided to forgo the trails, and as we were driving out of the park Rick commented how "snaky" the area was. Then, up ahead a couple of vehicles were stopped in the road. It was a fairly large rattlesnake blocking the way. Whew, that was too close for comfort!

---

[12] The war of the rebellion: a compilation of the official records of the Union and Confederate armies. ; Series 1 - Volume 23 (Part II) Author: United States. War Dept., John Sheldon Moody, Calvin Duvall Cowles, Frederick Caryton Ainsworth, Robert N. Scott, Henry Martyn Lazelle, George Breckenridge Davis, Leslie J. Perry, Joseph William Kirkley (online) p. 946

[13] Fold3 compiled records for William H. Van Meter, 6th Kentucky regiment Co. H

September 1863 – Kentucky AND Georgia

LEYDEN'S ARTILLERY: Was "one of the most splendid batteries in the services" as noted in the Atlanta Intelligencer newspaper. On September 9th 1863, Company A (Barnes Georgia Battery) was among the 2,100 men stationed at Cumberland Gap, Kentucky. Lt. William R. McEntire, in the unit, witnessed what was thought of as a horrible decision made by the commanding officer.[14] The unconditional surrender by General Frazier of Mississippi who was in charge, caused an outcry for further investigation in the matter. Frazier was ordered to hold ground until re-enforcements came – but instead he surrendered to the Federals without so much as a weapon drawn. With truce flags flying, Lt. McEntire did not think the situation was desperate and when the enemy positioned their weapons, he aimed and fired a cannon at them, against orders. He was immediately placed under arrest and on Sept. 7th sent home to Atlanta first (being a Mason gave him this privilege) before going to the officers prison on Johnson's Island, Lake Erie Ohio[15]. Some of the soldiers were able to escape but many were sent to Fort Douglas, Illinois prison camp.[16] Parts of Leyden's artillery Companies A & E were captured. Prisons on both sides were brutal, but toward the end of the war, the worst was Andersonville in mid-Georgia.

---

[14] The daily intelligencer. (Atlanta, Ga.) 1858-1868, September 23, 1863, Image 2 GAhistoricalnewspapers.com.

[15] Confederate Veteran p 389 October 1920 CD-rom

[16] Per Roster of Company A 9th Georgia Battalion, Leyden's Artillery
https://www.academia.edu/7641832/Company_A_9th_Battalion_Georgia_Artillery_Leydens_Artillery

CLARKE: July 2nd, 2016
ANDERSONVILLE PRISON

On the way to Americus, Georgia, Rick and I stopped by the notoriously horrible Andersonville prison, where thousands of Union soldiers were inadequately taken care of, and died in the years 1863 thru 1865. We walked into the Visitor's center next to the new POW museum at Andersonville. Luckily we were indoors in the cool air-conditioned complex, this scorching July day, in order to hear the guide talk about the prison. Standing next to a famous descriptive painting by Thomas O'Dea of the prison, solemnly, the small group gathered to listen to all of the horrors that the Union soldiers went through. The painting told the story, as we saw that the prison was completely outdoors in a field with guard's towers every few feet atop the long tall wooden fence that surrounded many acres. Andersonville quickly became over-crowded, and many died and were buried here.

After the talk, we saw what was remaining of the grounds. It was very hot that day, as I am sure it was over 150 years ago. We saw the tiny creeks that converged, and were now dried up, which was their only water supply for the prisoners. Due to the overcrowding of the prison, thousands died from not only starvation, but contaminated water causing dysentery and disease. We saw examples of the small tents which was all they had for shelter in the Stockade. In the hallway was a picture of the different Civil War prisons, including Camp Douglas, where part of Leyden's artillery ended up. Known as the "North's Andersonville", it was said to have the worst fatality of all the Northern prisons housing Confederates.[17]

LEYDEN'S ARTILLERY: On September 14th, Leyden has been assigned to Peebles command (Company D) under Colonel Trigg which fought in the Battle of Chickamauga, Georgia on

---

[17] Camp Douglas, Chicago: https://en.wikipedia.org/wiki/Camp_Douglas_(Chicago)

September 19th and 20th. McMurtrey writes on two days earlier, that they marched for 29 days from Virginia. It was company C, D and E that fought in the battle[18], which was a Confederate victory. General Longstreet, whom Leyden's artillery was assigned, came in the nick of time to save the day. Robert was probably at camp in Lafayette that day, awaiting word of the outcome.

Clarke: 2013: Monuments and Mud
150th Battle of Chickamauga

Several years ago Rick went shopping for a new vehicle after his Saturn "died". He would not be able to get another new Saturn because they had been discontinued. After meticulous research, we went to visit a nearby Toyota dealership to check out a small to mid-sized pickup truck that would be able to fit in our garage. He test drove a silver truck. He was very satisfied with it, and when questioned said that "color doesn't matter". As I was surveying the parking lot, I spotted a vehicle that stood out from the crowd, so I pointed and said, "What about that one?" Ultimately Rick decided that color did matter, and drove off the lot the proud owner of a bright metallic blue Toyota Tacoma.

Off in the blue truck, we headed very late to North Georgia to participate in the 150th anniversary of the Battle of Chickamauga. Five years earlier a former U.S. Vice President had spoken about his ancestor, Sam of the 12th New Hampshire regiment. We passed through the town of LaFayette, named for the French Revolutionary, and where the base of Leyden's artillery was residing during the battle.

MISSISSIPPI 27th. In one of the regimental accounts it states that before the Battle of Chickamauga, they were in and

---

[18] Letters from Lucinda dated Sept. 16 1863.

out of the caves on the sides of the mountains, chasing the enemy scouts, and that rations were low.[19] Chickamauga was a Confederate victory.

December 1863 – Cobb's Legion Calvary

HUFF: On December 19th Jeremiah writes from Piney River in the cold mountains 30 miles above Lynchburg, in Amherst County. They will soon head toward Fineycastle, Botetort. He then writes his wife Elizabeth from Peddler Mill, Amherst County near blue ridge 18 miles from Lynchburg Under Lt. Benet in VA. His mare is not doing well and is no longer fit for service. He mentions a possible furlough in spring to come home to get another horse. The horse was likely hurt from toting 40 pounds of ammunition from Manassas per his earlier letter signed Your Love Till Death, J.E. Huff. He says Christmas will be dull, and cold but he has plenty of blankets and they can eat as they please. He is glad that he does not have to go on picket or hear the bugles at all times of the night. By January 4th, they have a room to stay in. He had left the regiment a month ago, Dec 8th, and had not heard from them. Horses have stable. Staying at Sam Richeson's – about 7 men. Talked of eating cabbage, potatoes, cornbread cake and apples, and gaining lots of weight at 185 becoming fat. All he is doing is feeding 3 horses, but it's better than being on picket. There was snow in the higher elevations and it is very cold there. The people there are Baptist, and his "own folks couldn't treat him better than they do here". The horse's name is Nelly Gray.[20]

---

[19] R.A. Jarman, 27th Regimental History Ibid. – No 48-2
[20] Letters from Jeremiah Huff of Cobb's Legion to his wife Elizabeth per Atlanta History Center Kenan Archives

Lincoln's Cottage at Old Soldiers Home near Washington DC – on left see President Lincoln and his horse, "Old Bob"[21]

---

[21] Old Bob – Wikipedia https://en.wikipedia.org/wiki/Old_Bob *(photo taken while touring the Old Soldiers Home in 2018)*

ANDERSONVILLE—VIEW FROM THE MAIN GATE.

Pauline D'Alvigny Campbell – Civil War Nurse

Harper's Weekly Andersonville View from the Main Gate

Pauline D'Alvigny Campbell – Civil War Nurse

Chapter 6: Fortifying Our Place-Jan-July 20th 1864

"For thou art my rock and my fortress. Deliver me, O my God, out of the hand of the wicked, out of the hand of the unrighteous and cruel man." Psalm 71:3b-4 (KJV)

LEYDEN'S ARTILLERY: While Pauline was overseeing the farm, and taking care of the children, Robert was stationed in Hickory, NC around April 20th. They were then sent back to Saltville around May 13th. According to McMurtrey it took them 5 days to make the trip back into Virginia. They remained in Saltville at least through May 30th. McMurtrey wrote his wife, and was wondering about the whereabouts of General Johnston[1]. In the meantime, Pauline had not received a letter from Robert in many months, so she probably would be keeping up with as much news as possible, as the war was drawing closer to her home.

MISSISSIPPI 27th AND ORPHAN BRIGADE: In early 1864, the Mississippi 27th regiment was assigned to Hood's corps in Northern Georgia, near Dalton. Winter for most of the Confederate troops there, was a time of re-grouping, some down-time, and determining the next steps. There was snow on the ground, which led to snowball fights within the camps, as mentioned by both the Mississippi 27th: and the Kentucky Orphans, stationed there.[2] Then, it was announced to the Orphan brigade, that their next campaign commander would be

---

[1] Mrs. Johnston, Letters from Lucinda – dated May 30th 1864 from James to Lucinda from Saltville VA.

[2] R.A. Jarman, Full text History of Company K, 27th Mississippi Infantry No. 51. Online version/Aberdeen examiner p1-2 and Lt. Lot D. Young, or Paris KY, "Reminiscences of a Solder of the Orphan Brigade (Electronic edition) University of North Carolina at Chapel Hill 2004 p75

General Johnston, and this greatly lifted their spirits.[3]   By this time Private Van Meter had returned to duty, from an extended illness of 6 months. He was assigned to duty as sharpshooter at Rockyface Ridge[4]. In the spring the company began digging trenches. The Orphans had a reputation for being as Trojans, as it was to them a pleasure to even dig "plumb through to China, if old Tecomseh (Sherman) will give us time". Time was of essence as the "sly fox", as they called him was heading their way.[5] Nevertheless, they got a short reprieve before the Battle of Resaca in mid-May.

Union troops, inching closer to Atlanta, began their attack on the Confederates entrenched in the hilly mountains of Kennesaw, north of Marietta. The Battle of Kennesaw on June 27th, however, was eventually a Southern victory under General Joseph Johnston. Southern casualties were 442 and Union losses were around 2,000.[6]

CLARKE: Year of 2012: Kennesaw Mountain

Regarding Kennesaw, we met an author who had written a fictional book based on a true story about ghosts she saw at Kennesaw Mountain. One evening around dusk, she looked up and saw a Union soldier, and she confirmed with the park that there were no re-enactors present that day.[7] Rick and I decided to tour the Battlefield later that year. We walked the trail towards the famous "Cheatham's Hill", up the path, past the Confederate earthworks, and looked down the hill. We could

---

[3] L.D Young, Orphan Brigade p 75 from "Documenting the American South", UNC Chapel Hill Libraries

[4] Ibid. Co 6 of Orphans was assigned to be sharpshooters.

[5] Confederate Veteran Magazine on CD June 1922 "How the Orphans learned to Dig", page 212

[6] John Bowman, "Chronicles of the War"World Publications Group 2005 p 311 Battle of Kennesaw Mountain

[7] Lois Helmers & Gerald Harding Gunn, "The Ghost of Kennesaw Mountain" (Badgley Publishing co. Canal Winchester Ohio 2011 and speech by Lois Helmers.

imagine how brutal it was for the Union forces to charge up the hill in the open grassy knoll being easy targets in plain sight of the Confederate troops. Sherman was determined to get beyond Kennesaw Mountain to ultimately reach Atlanta. The Battle of Kennesaw was a confederate victory under Joseph E. Johnston. In spite of this triumph for the Southern soldiers, however, General Johnston would soon be replaced by General Hood.

It soon became clear that the Rebels were outnumbered. General Johnston eagerly awaited re-enforcements, as in spite of their losses, General Sherman's army pressed in on Marietta, forcing a Confederate retreat. President of the Confederate States, Jefferson Davis, a West Point military graduate himself, warned Johnston not to let Sherman cross the Chattahoochee. Those re-enforcements never came. As we started out of the park, back around the earthworks, something caught our attention and we stopped dead in our tracks. Ghosts? No, it was deer, so close we could almost walk up and touch them.

CLARKE: Crossing the Covered Bridge Roswell Georgia

The city of Roswell sits right on the Chattahoochee River. We took a tour of the remains of the Roswell mill and apartment homes of the mill workers, who in 1864 were discovered by Sherman's troops. After walking across a covered bridge over Vickery creek, a tributary of the Chattahoochee River, we viewed the ruins of the mills burned by Sherman. We saw some apartments built by Mr. King who founded the mill in 1840, called "The Bricks". This is where the millworkers lived. It still stands today. [8]

On July 5th, Sherman sent Garrard's cavalry to find a good place to cross the Chattahoochee over toward Atlanta.

---

[8] Macallan, http://thebricksroswell.com/history.html "The Bricks, History of the Bricks" 2006 Macallan Residential

What he found was the Roswell mill that was still making Confederate grey uniforms. The mill was operated mostly by around 400 women. Orders the next day came down from Sherman to take supplies for Union hospitals from the cotton mill, and take all the workers, male or female prisoner. At first they were sent to Marietta, but ultimately he sent the women, some with children North by train.[9] Pauline was at her home at Peachtree creek with her three children.

PAULINE: "Everything went well for us until July 6th, 1864. Our troops began to retreat from the Chattahoochee River and men were digging trenches and fortifying our place".

Sherman's sights were on Atlanta, and he was elated to capture undefended Roswell, without even a skirmish. One step closer, Sherman began to cross the Chattahoochee River and had troops situated along the northern side alongside Peachtree Creek on one of its tributaries. An account by a local citizen regarding, July 10, 1864: "This has been a sad day for our people", as the Union Army was fast approaching stores and hospitals began closing down and people started leaving.[10] Many of the Roswell mill workers were put on a train northbound and many were never heard from again.[11]

---

[9] Maggie McLean, post of 5/10/2014; Civil War Women: Exile of the Roswell Mill Women; https://www.civilwarwomenblog.com/exile-of-the-roswell-mill-women/
[10] Franklin M. Garrett, *Atlanta and Environs: A Chronicle of Its People and Events* (Athens: University of Georgia Press, 1954), Volume I p600
[11] Madigan, Kevin, Atlanta Journal Constitution site: July 30, 2015 "Who are the Lost Mill Workers of Roswell" per https://www.ajc.com/lifestyles/who-are-the-lost-mill-workers-roswell/h6GemkUA8kauCuYsn26vSJ/

CLARKE: July 1994 - Shooting the Hooch

It was a common thing in the summer to "shoot the hooch", in a raft or tube. Rick and I met at the Lightshine Sunday School class for Singles at the Norcross First United Methodist Church. I had been attending about 2 years and was involved in many of their activities, plus was part of the Activity planning committee. One hot, sultry, summer day in July, a group of us met to go "Floating Down the Chattahoochee River". We arrived at the point of departure in Marietta, off Johnson's creek. This was my first trip on a raft down the river. Rick and I ended up navigating the muddy waters together, happily ever after.

PAULINE: "Then I was obliged to go into Atlanta, leaving all behind me except one load of provisions and some clothing, me, with my little family sitting on top of the loaded wagon"

Pauline was forced from her home, with 3 small children in tow. She left her farm and all she owned to seek refuge in Atlanta, which was several miles east, and where her father, Dr. Noel was tending to more and more wounded soldiers.

While many civilians were leaving Atlanta, Pauline was headed there with three young children from the ages of two to seven years old. Evalina was the eldest, Helen around five years old, and the "baby" was Robert Jr. She made her way to stay in a room in back of the Medical College Hospital, were her father was serving as surgeon in Atlanta. When the War began, Dr. D'Alvigny had offered the services of his family as nurses, at no charge. At the time she didn't realize just how much she would be needed there. This was just before a battle would ensue near her farm.

How devastating it must have been to give up your home and belongings, not knowing if there will be a home to go back to. The Huff's lived near the Campbell's and left their home after the Battle of Peachtree Creek which occurred July 20th 1864 near their home. Sarah Huff was eight years old at this time, and wrote a memoir at the age of 80 years old about her life and experiences. Sarah's mother, Elizabeth was Pauline Campbell's best friend. They both had children around the same age.

CLARKE October 2012: The Cannons on Collier Road

Rick and I were driving out to the cemetery to put flowers on the grave of Rick's mother, Jean, who had passed away earlier in the year. He mentioned to me, as we were heading down Collier Road, that he frequented a park in his youth with actual Cannons from the Battle of Peachtree Creek. I had never been to the park before and wanted to take a look. We found the entrance among the trees and it was not well advertised. There were plaques there, but no cannons. We wondered what had happened to them...but there was Peachtree Creek and a walking trail now called "the Beltline". A feeling of accomplishment arose as we walked along the trail. We had belonged to a railroad passenger advocate association called GARP (Georgia Association of Railroad Passengers). They had asked me to help plan one of their events in Atlanta. This was when the Beltline was in the planning stages, and we had a speaker to come and tell us all about it. Surprisingly, we decided to hold the event at the hotel where the daughter-in-law of our dear friends, Pearl and Jerry, so happened to be employed at. We found that out after we selected the location. The meeting was well-attended and a success.

MISSISSIPPI 27th: Even after the Kennesaw victory, Joe Johnston could not keep the Union from entrenching themselves further and further into Georgia. General Joe Johnston had been relieved of his command by President Jefferson Davis. This came at quite a shock to the morale of the troops, who greatly admired Johnston. General Hood, who had been wounded, and lost a leg, was put in charge, as he was more aggressive in manner. General Walthall was promoted to be in command of an entire Division. Also the 27th Mississippi Regiment was assigned to the now Brigadier General Brantley and its name changed to Brantley's brigade.[12]

ATLANTA: As battles escalated in Georgia, the citizen's anxieties mounted. Atlanta became a major hub for the ill and wounded soldiers in the spring and summer of 1864. "Great numbers of sick and wounded soldiers, daily arriving at the passenger depot, were met by the ladies of our first families, with baskets filled with delicacies".[13] Sarah Huff, whose family stayed behind, writes, "45,000 Confederate soldiers marched by on Marietta Street, just across the railroad and the valley from Huff House". Music had filled the air one night when it was learned of the fate of General Johnston, and many were sorrowful over it. She writes in her memoirs, "At midnight when the old Atlanta watchman's voice rang out: "Twelve o'clock, and all's well!" the clear-hearing statesmen of the Southland heard the doom bells ringing the death knell of the Southern Confederacy." The battle of Peachtree Creek was in the afternoon of July 20th 1864. It was a devastating Union victory. Hood's army had 5,000 casualties.[14] Churches, homes and farms were destroyed. The very next day Elizabeth Huff was weeping when the Union officers came and told her to leave

---

[12] Boatner III, Mark M. *The Civil War Dictionary* (New York: Vintage Books, 1988) 82, 888

[13] https://archive.org/stream/emory1867/emory1867_djvu.txt Full Text Full text of "Atlanta City Directory Co.'s Greater Atlanta (Georgia) city directory ... including Avondale, Buckhead ... and all immediate suburbs "

[14] John Bowman, Chronicles, Ibid. p336

her home.[15] Sarah wrote a poem about her Mother leaving their home behind as follows:

What Mother Carried Along

Home ties must break
But what could they take?
As they hurried and scurried along?
South my Mother to save the best
Of the things that she possessed
She could not carry much along.
Grandfather's clock ticked in the hall,
Grandmother's picture decked the wall,
To these did cherished thoughts belong –
But the battle roar entered the door
She could not carry these treasures along.
Into her bookcase Mother did look,
Dropping hot tears on each loved book
She was a lover of learning and song,
But the cannon's "boom" rocked the room
She could not carry her books along.
As little children around her flocked,
She thought of a cradle in which they were rocked
Motherhood welled in her heart so strong.
Dire was need as she refugeed.
By wagon and train and back home again,
But she carried their cradle along![16]

---

[15] Sarah Huff, My 80 Years, Ibid p.10-14 online version at

[16] "Sarah Huff Papers", James G. Kenan Research Center Manuscript Collections MSS 120 includes Poems

Tanyard Creek at the Battle of Peachtree Creek July 1864

Pauline D'Alvigny Campbell – Civil War Nurse

Chapter 7 : July 22, 1864
The Battle of Atlanta

"For every battle of the warrior is with confused noise, and garments rolled in blood; but this shall be with burning and fuel of fire." Isaiah 9:5 (KJV)

PAULINE: "Two days later shot and shell began to fall on the city. Women were frightened to death almost. You could see them running with hands just out of the dough, bareheaded, the children crying and not a thing saved in their houses."

CLARKE: Touring Luke's Old Neighborhood

Rick and I rode around an East Atlanta neighborhood, near Moreland Avenue where his Uncle Luke had lived and where soldiers had once fought. It was July 22, 2012 and exactly 148 years since the Battle of Atlanta. The theme for the annual event was "From Civil War to Civil Rights" and commemorated the battle with various activities including a walking tour. This wasn't your typical battlefield. On a drizzly day, the tour guide, and his dog, Walker, a sweet-looking beagle, took a small group of us over hilly terrain that was once covered with trees and now was full of nice homes, shops and parks. Some of the tall Oaks were all that remained of Sherman's 1864 assault on the outskirts of Atlanta. We walked up the very paths, where Union soldiers took the higher ground and the Confederates charged up hill. Within a few blocks we saw where Union General McPherson was shot and killed. A commemorative wreath had been placed near the plaque, surrounded by resident's homes. The tour ended on Leggett's Hill, where 8,000 Confederates and 3,000 Union soldiers died. We stood in a gas station lot, overlooking the busy Interstate I-20. A Union victory with many casualties, as Sherman had out-maneuvered the tiring

Confederates, the latter being unable to defend their city. As we drove around the area, Rick remembered his Aunts and Uncles lived here, and he pointed out the Methodist church they attended. He recalls at that time they had to have bars put on the windows. The area is much nicer now.

The Battle of Atlanta: Shot & Shell

Federal troops were being taken to the local hospitals, including the Atlanta Medical College, where Dr. Logan was in charge and Dr. D'Alvigny was serving as surgeon.   In the meantime, many residents were waiting to take the very trains out, where troops were coming in. On the evening of July 20th, during the Battle of Peachtree Creek a few miles west of Atlanta, other residents were scurrying about Atlanta. There was a story told of a child dying as her family crossed the streets, but since this has been questioned by historians. [1] Many of the several thousand civilians still in the city were taken by surprise at the start of shelling as no warning was given.[2]

The shelling continued. Sherman's army, on the outskirts of Atlanta, continued targeting the city. It became almost a daily routine to run to the bomb-proof shelters around town during bouts of shells raining on the homes and buildings. Pauline, who assisted her father as a nurse helped the wounded as they came in by train at the carshed from the main depot. Pauline stayed near the Atlanta Medical College. "Assisting" may have meant comforting or applying bandages, or steadying those about to have a leg amputated, or supplying the morphine. It may also mean dressing wounds, or helping a soldier write a final goodbye to a loved one. [3] The carshed served as a triage distributing place. Due to the battle, the wounded were sent

---

[1] Steven Davis, "The Yankees and What They Did to Us" Ibid, p 107-108

[2] Atlanta History Center: Atlanta Historical Society, Inc. A Journal of Georgia and the South, VOL XLV H 4 2003.

along the rail lines to other locations prior to the upcoming battle. Only the most seriously injured remained in the city.[4]

PAULINE: "I was lodged in a house back of the Medical College and the first day 24 shells fell around me."

Pauline's father lived a couple of blocks from the Medical college but she was staying in another house behind the college when thousands of wounded soldiers began coming in.[5] Some shell shots strayed into Atlanta from Peachtree Creek, but the heavy fighting in the city began on July 22nd when the Battle of Atlanta began. Pauline's friend Sarah Huff mentions in her memoirs that the day after the battle of Atlanta, homes and farms were demolished, and the ground appeared "red with blood".[6] One of her neighbors, the Edwards, displayed a British flag on the Huff house near Peachtree Creek, in trying to save their home from being burned.[7]

According to Sarah, "During the battle the bullets fell thickly in the yard of 'the Atlanta Medical College where Dr. D'Alvigny was operating. His daughter, Pauline D'Alvigny Campbell, who was assisting her father, narrowly escaped being hit several times, since on account of the intense heat the operating table had been carried out into the shade of several nearby trees."[8] Meanwhile, General Hood watched part of the battle on a hill in Oakland cemetery.[9]

---

[4] Franklin Garrett, Atlanta Environs, Vol 1 p530

[5] Sarah Huff, "Mrs. Robert Campbell, A Heroine of the Hospital, booklet from the Old Jail Museum & Archive in Barnesville Ga, written by Sarah Huff. P7-8; My 80 Years page 14

[6] Sarah Huff, Ibid. p 15

[7] Sarah Huff, 80 years, Ibid. p13

[8] Sarah Huff, 80 years Ibid. p16

[9] Barry L. Brown and Gordon R. Elwell, "Crossroads of Conflict" A Guide to Civil War Sites in Georgia. P. 86

PAULINE: "I then moved nearer the center of the city. The next Sunday I was sitting by a window, looking out at the passing crowd, trying to get baby to sleep, when a piece of shell passed through that window and passing through a chair, on which I had been sitting, it went through the floor. That was close call #1"

Day after day, shell after shell, more civilians were wounded, killed or barely escaped the onslaught. The shells did not discriminate – confederate soldiers, a lady with her little boy in the yard and a mule fell victim.[10] People headed for bomb-proofs. Pauline had some narrow escapes herself. Shells bursting, bullets whizzing by, it was a dangerous time. Pauline was "as much exposed as any soldier engaged in active battle".[11] On most Sunday's the citizens attended church services, including Father O'Reilly's Church of the Immaculate Conception (Catholic) and the Trinity Methodist Church, as well as others. Pauline had to move due to the intense shelling, and at one point stayed at Dr. Willis Westmoreland's house, which was on Marietta Street.[12] After the War it was reported that the Westmoreland house was among many homes that were damaged.[13]

CLARKE: 2001: Blackhawk Down

For Hotlanta, New Year's Day 2001 was quite bone-chilling, in several ways. It was a day that we'll never forget. The temperature dipped below freezing, but nonetheless, Rick

---

[10] Robert J. Campbell Diary (not Pauline's husband). NC Press Chapel Hill 1938 and "Atlanta History Center"; Atlantia Historical Society, Inc. a Journal of Georgia and the South vol XLV H 4 2003.

[11] Sarah Huff, 80 years, Ibid. P11-12

[12] Sarah Huff, "Mrs. Robert Campbell, A Heroine of the Hospital, booklet from the Old Jail Museum & Archive in Barnesville Ga, written by Sarah Huff. P7-8

[13] Stephen Davis, What the Yankees, Ibid, p162

and I ventured out to meet friends, pulling up at the big red "V" sign for lunch. The vintage restaurant is famous for their greasy chili dogs, and onion rings, literally dripping with oil, among other Southern cuisine. As Rick and I are native Atlantans (Rick being a 7th generation resident) we heard many stories from our parents who frequented the college hangout in their youth. Rick's father Tom and my father, Ray, both attended Georgia Tech, a well-renown engineering and technical university nearby. The drive in restaurant was a favorite hangout for many Atlantans.

After lunch Rick and I decided to find the street named for the doctor: Dalvigney Street, not far from there. We had never been in that section before. I had my camera with me and thought it would be neat to take a picture of the street sign. We drove over the railroad tracks we cruised in our brick-red Saturn. Apparently we were on the wrong side of the tracks, because we passed by vacant houses on the left, a few miles down the road. Then we had a sinking feeling, as we approached a two-way stop, and saw men in trench "coats" that is. I wish it really were Tommy Lee Jones and Will Smith, from the *"Men in Black"* movie to protect us, but no such luck.

We took a right turn (in hindsight a wrong turn) towards D'Alvigney Street. I could see the street sign up ahead and had my camera poised to take a picture, when we saw them. Swiftly, I dropped my camera in my lap, on purpose, so it could not be seen. All of a sudden, there was a crowd of men walking determined to go towards our vehicle. (By the way, the car was still in motion, slowly moving along the street). Rick was trying not to hit any of the men, as they were approaching and yelling out to us. Rick asked how many are on your side? I exclaimed, "I think about 20, and they are touching the car!!" Luckily, Rick always locks the doors when travelling. Rick rounded the corner onto D'Alvigney Street. The camera remained in my lap. He circled the block, away from the group, and then headed back towards the exact same intersection. "What are you doing!!", I frantically shouted. "We can't go back that way!" Rick, turned his head, looked at me with fear and determination in his eyes, and said, "We have to...that's the only way I know how to get outta here!!". I cried out repeatedly, "run the stop sign!!" He retorted, "I intend to!!" So, he did, and we were then safely on our way back home, praising God all the way, while breathing sighs of relief. I felt that we had somehow ended up in the movie, *"Blackhawk Down"* and as intense as *"Judgement Night"*. Rick later found out the place was called "Buttermilk Bottoms" by the locals.

CLARKE: 2002 – Reunion Day Trip – Cyclorama and Oakland Cemetery

Rick arranged a bus for the family reunion on the 2nd day, to visit both the Cyclorama and Oakland cemetery on a day trip. First, we stopped at Grant Park, and saw the mega mural painting by Weis Snell depicting July 22nd, The Battle of Atlanta[14]. It has been told that when Clark Gable came to tour the Cyclorama at the *Gone with the Wind* movie premiere, he made a comment to the artist that there was no likeness of "Rhett Butler", jokingly. The artist, however, fixed it up so one of the dead Union soldiers resembled Rhett.[15]

After seeing the Texas Locomotive (the train that was chasing the General during Andrews Raid in 1862) which was also housed at the Cyclorama, our next stop was Oakland cemetery. The family was excited to see Charles and Noel's graves, and we all gathered round and sang a French song to commemorate the occasion. Later, after everyone had left and Rick and I were at home, I noticed there was a message on our answering machine. I played it and it sounded very garbled and rambled on and on. What kind of message is this, I thought.

---

[14] Gene Meier, Biograph of Weis C. Snell; http://www.askart.com/artist/Weis_C_Snell/11253987/Weis_C_Snell.aspx
[15] The Civil War Pickett, "Rhett Butler and the Atlanta Cyclorama"; http://civil-war-picket.blogspot.com/2009/12/rhett-butler-and-atlanta-cyclorama.html

Then I realized that it was us, the reunion group, standing around singing on the D'Alvigny plot. I laughed so hard! I had been wearing my cell phone on my belt and it accidently called our house!

Scene of General McPherson's Death [16]

---

[16] *Scene of McPherson's death*. Atlanta Georgia United States, ca. 1894. Chicago, Ill.: The Puritan Press Co. Photograph. https://www.loc.gov/item/2003663128/.

Pauline D'Alvigny Campbell – Civil War Nurse

Chapter 8: Dog Days in Atlanta: August 1864

For that which befalleth the sons of men befalleth beasts; even one thing befalleth them: as the one dieth, so dieth the other; yea, they have all one breath; so that a man hath no preeminence above a beast: for all [is] vanity. Ecclesiastes 3:19-20 (KJV)

PAULINE: "One night they shelled the city every two minutes. A shell killed a new born baby and its mother in a house adjoining mine. I hastened into a bomb-proof as fast as possible. As I entered the door to this shelter, a sixty-pounder fell almost at my feet. Suppose it had burst, where would I have been?"

Carrie Berry is known for writing a diary when she was a child, living in the city of Atlanta during the War. Following are excerpts from this diary written during the horrible month of August 1864 when the shelling was especially heavy. She writes almost daily and conveys the frequency and intensity of the shelling that Pauline was also in the midst of. She writes August 3rd that "this was my birthday, I was ten years old, but I did not have cake because times were too hard." On August 4th ,"the shells have been flying all day and we have stayed in the cellar". On Friday, August 5th: "We did not feel safe in our cellar, they fell so thick and fast". However, on Sunday she was able to go to church after having not attended for an entire month. The preacher at the Trinity Methodist church she and her Papa attended that day was Rev. Atticus Haygood. Two days later they were back in the cellar. By August 21st, their cellar was not safe anymore and they were forced to move. After the move on Tuesday August 23rd she writes, "the shells get worse and worse every day". Also she says that many fires were occurring in the city at this time. By Friday, August 26th, the "Yankees had left their brest works".[1]

HUFF: Mrs. Elizabeth Huff writes her Mother on August 21, 1864 as follows. "The shells come(s) whistling over and around us every day". Mr. Huff had made it home that Wednesday, very sick and almost ended up behind Yankee lines, but he found his way home. He attempted to get them out from their home, as "raiders" would destroy anything they had, and they had loaded stuff on the car, hoping to take a train to Newnan, which is 40 miles, and then to the Huff family, Jeramiah's parents. The houses near them haven't been hit yet, but they live in constant fear of the shelling.   Yanks have been shelling the "Marietta" street side more often. Effie Erwin Hudson's house has been hit 6 times. The Yanks breast works is in plain view. "Every one that passes the street they throw shells at them" so the Hudson's are afraid to even move out of their house. The Peter's Flour Mill near the railroad was also used as a bomb-shelter during the Siege of Atlanta.[2]

ATLANTA: Anton Kontz, only thirteen years old and one of D'alvigny's neighbors, was rambling down the streets, scanning the ground with his keen eyes. He was hoping to discover shell fragments or other material that would be helpful to the Confederate forces. Secretly, Anton wanted to join them in the fight but he was too young. Therefore he felt the need to help out any way he could. His buddy was with him, his dog, close by his side, sniffing the ground. Then in an instant a shell came whizzing by and exploded in front of him. Anton then realized that his dog was hit. Dr. D'Alvigny was coming around the corner and saw Anton crying hysterically. The concerned doctor

---

[1] "A Confederate Girl, The Diary of Carrie Berry, 1864", Edited by Christy Steele with Anne Todd; Blue Earth Books, Capstone Press, Mankato, MN, Copyright 2000, pages: 8-13)

[2] Sarah Huff Diary, Ibid. Chapter 14 p39

approached him hurriedly. Anton looked down upon his chest and his shirt was soaked with blood, and it was his own. D'Alvigny tended to the wound, and tried to calm him, saying it was only minor, that he would be OK, But Anton was more upset about his dog than himself. When the doctor left, Anton picked up his lifeless friend in his arms and headed off somewhere to bury his best friend.[3]

ATLANTA – August 8, 1864 – Not so Luckie

Solomon Luckie owned a shop on Alabama Street, near or at the Atlanta Hotel. Sometimes known as "Sam", Solomon was a well-known and liked man in the community. He was a businessman and one of the 40 or so free African-American people living in Atlanta during the time of the War. He was married to Nancy Cunningham and had a family of three children.[4]

Solomon was standing on the Northeast corner of Alabama Street and Whitehall Street (now Peachtree St.) when a shell struck a nearby lamppost. A fragment of the shell pierced through his leg and he went down in an instant. Quickly, some witnesses to the event, picked him up and carried him to Dr. D'Alvigny, who went to work on him immediately. He was given morphine and the mangled leg was amputated promptly. However, infection set in, and Solomon Luckie died shortly thereafter.

The lamppost was preserved and stood for many years as a reminder to all who passed, as several plaques were placed upon it by the United Daughters of the Confederacy. But none of the plaques mentioned Solomon or his fate. As of this

---

[3] Author unknown; Jan 24 1937 Atlanta Constitution "Monument of Service Left City and Long Life of Anton Louis Kontz"
[4] Luckie bio from Atlanta History Center:
http://ahc.galileo.usg.edu/ahc/view?docId=ead/ahc.VIS20-ead.xml

writing, the lamppost will be moved to the Atlanta History Center.

PAULINE: 'The next days news reached us that a courier had brought in letters. I had not had a letter from my husband in eight months. I resolved to go to the post office. Miss Thursa Fleming, now Mrs. Wright, accompanied me. Just as we reached the park, near where the Kimball house now stands, we heard the boom of cannon. We jumped into a nearby piazza. At the same moment an army wagon came dashing past from the depot and a piece of the shell passed through one of the mules and another piece cut its way through the skirt of my dress. The mule fell down but its rider was not hurt. We went on to the post office and I got a letter."

The Kimball House was built at Five Points on Whitehall Street during the Reconstruction period after the war and was a grand and glorious hotel of yellow brick with brown trim. Many businessmen, politicians, celebrities and the like attended this hot spot frequently. With 500 rooms, its claim to fame was that it was first building in Atlanta to have central heat and elevators[5]. Unfortunately in 1883 it accidently burned down. It was re-built and re-opened in 1885. Hugh T. Inman bought the Kimball house and gave it to his daughter, Ann, as a wedding gift in 1893.[6]

CLARKE: 1990's: Grandmother and The Inman Family

Rick's grandmother, Mildred Alexander Clarke Johnson, was a most hospitable and gracious lady. She always insisted upon make-up and lipstick when we visited her in the nursing home near the end of her days. She had told Rick when he was a

---

[5] https://en.wikipedia.org/wiki/Kimball_House_(Atlanta) - Description of the Kimball House (7/26/18)
[6] Kimball House, Ibid.

teenager, all about Dr. D'Alvigny. In fact, even when her mind was failing, she always lit up when we would mention the D'Alvigny name. Once, we were discussing family history, (more like an interrogation on our part), and she mentioned growing up and playing at the house of Mrs. U.T. Inman. We kept asking her, Who?, and in her elegant, whispering voice she replied...."You-T!, "You- T!!...then got rather upset when we didn't know who or what she was talking about. In fact we later realized it was Mrs. HUGH T. Inman that she was speaking of.. The Inmans were a well-known family who owned the exquisite Swan House Estate in Buckhead (near the Atlanta History Center) and at the time, not far from where Mildred lived. Mildred's mother, Emma had worked for them in her youth. Mildred recalled going with her mother from time to time and playing on the marble floors. Emma Bohler Alexander was a strong sometimes brash lady, who once got upset with her neighbors and threw raw fish bones out the window into their yard. Emma lived in a middle-class neighborhood and everyone would gawk when a limo would pick her up from time to time to take her to visit Josephine Inman Richardson. Josephine was Hugh T. Inman's other daughter. She and Emma were around the same age and knew each other well. Emma even named one of her own children Josephine, Mildred's older sister. No one living knows how the Inmans were connected, only that Emma had known the Inmans from way back and had once worked for them. Milledge Alexander, Emma's husband, had once worked at "Inman Yards" railway. Also, Robert Campbell did work for Inman Dry goods store on Pryor Street.[7]

ATLANTA: July & August 1864: Snail Mail

During the siege of Atlanta and in the months of July and August, it was very difficult, and nearly impossible to reach anyone in Atlanta by letter, or for the citizens who stayed behind to get a letter. Pauline, however, was determined with a spirit

---

[7] Family papers on Robert Campbell

that would not fail, risking her life to reach the Post Office when she heard of letters coming in. It had been many months since she had a letter from her husband. In her memoirs Sallie Clayton mentioned that she could "get no letters through to Atlanta (she had left early July), nor receive any". They had to rely on the papers who would tell of Atlanta citizens being wounded or even killed, but listed no names, only mentioning streets.[8]

CLARKE: Back in Time At Nash Farms

The very first major re-enactment I did was in McDonough, Georgia at a place called Nash Farms. It was the "Battle of Atlanta" because there is really no place in the actual city of Atlanta to have a re-enactment. Since I mentioned that Rick and I don't do camping, we stayed at a local hotel. I had my new period style 1860's dress that I got at a shop in Chickamauga, and a hat, but had not purchased re-enactor shoes or socks. I was wearing a normal pair of Mary Jane style shoes with straps, trampling over thick waves of grass, crossing the field. Being a civilian re-enactor with the large hoop dress, puts you back in time. You actually know what it feels like to "send off" your man to battle, and worry whether they would get hurt. Although no real bullets are used, there are dangers to re-enacting, such as heatstroke and heaven-forbid, a heart attack while fighting. I'm always relieved when Rick makes it back safely after the "Battle". I can hardly understand what the women in the Civil War had to go through, the challenges of taking care of their family and the fear and waiting for letters, or some kind of word from their husbands. It was hot that day, but Rick made it fine through his first battle. Before the close of day I had been bitten by a spider

---

[8] Robert S. Davis, Jr. Sarah Conley Clayton, "Requiem for Lost City (Civil War Georgia (Mercer University Press 1999),account of Sallie Clayton p 120

or something, and there was a large whelp on my foot. It took several trips to the doctor to heal.

The next time I went to Nash Farms, I had the proper attire and was so happy to wear my new gown to the Ball. They had lively music going, songs, and someone calling the dance called the Virginia Reel. I recall learning this dance in Mrs. Hayes fourth grade class and can vividly hear in my mind, the recording saying, "Now everybody go forward and back". One time during the day-battle I was able to join in on a group of women playing their mountain dulcimers. I had brought mine too. We were just strumming away by the tents at the camp. I have to say that Nash Farms is my favorite re-enactment to participate in, and I have very fond memories there that I will always treasure, even in spite of the insect bites.

Photo of Display at Food Court, Mall of Georgia,
In the lower right-hand corner is Solomon Luckie

1850 - 25 "free persons of color" lived in Atlanta, though o through the consent of the city council. One such person wa Luckie Solomon, a barber who conducted his business in the Atlanta Hotel. Unfortunately for Luckie, he was killed by shelling during Sherman's siege of Atlanta.

St.

Luckie Solomon

From the Display with permission by the Mall of Georgia in Buford

Pauline D'Alvigny Campbell – Civil War Nurse

Chapter 9: Atlanta: TAKEN

If it be so, our God whom we serve is able to deliver us from the burning fiery furnace, and he will deliver us out of thine hand.. Daniel 3:17 KJV

PAULINE: "After Atlanta was taken a Yankee drove up to the door and gave me my choice, to go north or south, that "no rebel could remain." I told him I would go south where gentlemen were found."

In the major cities up North the word was out to the newspapers, "General Sherman has taken Atlanta". Per Mary Rawson's diary of September 2nd 1864, she states "The day has closed and is numbered with those past and gone, and the moon once more shines over sleeping, silent Atlanta". [1] Hood evacuated Atlanta on the night of September 1st. Soldiers marched out of the city and the ammunitions and other supplies were blown up by Confederate forces under the command of the General.

Around noon the next day, on Sept. 2nd, the Federals came and the Mayor of Atlanta surrendered the city. It was mentioned on September 5th by the provost Marshall that the first evacuations would be of those whose husbands were fighting and would go south, which would take place in the next five days.[2] Then later, the non-essential civilians would be ordered to leave and given the choice North or South. Some civilians of use to the Union were allowed to stay.[3] Since Pauline's husband was still fighting, I would assume she would be in the first category and one of the first to be sent out of the

---

[1] A.A. Hoehling, Last Train p 426-7 as told by Dr. James Patton, Princeton Indiana
[2] Atlanta and the Civil War; Evacuation of All Citizens; https://en.wikipedia.org/wiki/Atlanta_in_the_American_Civil_War#Evacuation_of_all_civilians_(September_8%E2%80%9321,_1864)
[3] https://warwashere.com/category/federal-occupation-of-atlanta/ "War Was Here" evacuation of Atlanta after Federals took occupation

city. Her father remained as he was needed to tend to the Union soldiers, and hired by the Federals. His pay was $100 by the Union army.[4] Pauline was also needed in the South at the Medical college hospital that had moved to Milner, Georgia under Dr. Willis Westmoreland.

A Union soldier writes home that on Sept. 2nd his was the first regiment to arrive in Atlanta. He mentioned that most houses had shell-damage, some even being "riddled" with shells. He described the bomb-proof shelters and heard that 100 citizens had been killed.[5]

PAULINE: "He carried us to the carshed at 9 o'clock in the morning. At 12 my little children were crying for bread and I had none to give them. A young solider, camped in the park, hearing their cries, came to us and said, he might be a hated Yankee, but he still had heart enough to give a little child something to eat. "Will you accept it?" said he. What could I do but accept the food?"

A Union doctor, Dr. Patterson from Indiana, describes an incident near the fortifications South of Atlanta on September 5th. He said that a young woman was "skinning" a cow that was dead on the side of the road, and a young child with her, of around age six or seven, was hungrily eating the raw meat. The scene shook the doctor up, as he described it as the most pitiful that the "poor children" are starving[6].

PAULINE" "At 4 o'clock the train started and we were stopped at East Point, for half an hour still surrounded by guards."

---

[4] Union Fee bill for Dr. D'Alvigny per the Atlanta History Center

[5] A.A. Hoehling *Last Train, Train from Atlanta*, Stratford Press, New York 1958. p.435

[6] A.A. Hoehling, *Last Train from Atlanta*, Ibid.. p445

Previously, Sherman had instructed his troops to destroy railroads up and down the line to prevent supplies in hopes of debilitating the Southern forces, and forcing surrender. He had cut the rail lines between the city called "Rough and Ready" and Jonesboro to cut supplies to the Confederacy. East Point was to the North of Rough and Ready. By order of Gen. Hood, Confederate troops were spread out in the Southern outskirts of Atlanta, in hopes to prevent the Federals from tearing up tracks on the Macon & Western Railroad. Confederate General Stephen D Lee was stationed in East Point. Union General Howard was instructed to cross east towards Jonesboro, near the Flint River, just before the battle would commence on August 31st. The route he took is the present day path known as Highway 138 which stretches from Fairburn, through Riverdale.[7]

CLARKE: 70's: Tap-Dancing all Around

When I was 9 years old, I attended the dance class of the Jean Morris Studio in East Point, Georgia. We only lived a few miles from there at the time on the outskirts of the city of Atlanta, near the Lakewood Fairgrounds. I recall standing in front of the mirror in a line of young girls, doing my Plie's and Releve's of ballet, but my favorite type of dance was tap. I recall one snazzy jazz recital where I was tapping away in my red-sequined outfit. I was also a milk maid in the production of the "Wizard of Oz". The movie came out the same year, in 1939, as Gone With The Wind. At Cleveland Avenue elementary, my fourth grade teacher had us doing the Virginia Reel in class. That was so

---

[7] J. Britt, McCarley, *The Battle of Jonesboro*" Atlanta Historical Society Journal Fall of 1984 "The Battle of Jonesboro"

much fun. I loved it!   By the time I was eleven years old, we had moved to Riverdale. The love of dance continued in my life, as I took a ballroom dance class at Fred Astaire studios in my twenties along with my Mother, Judy, who also loved to dance . I learned the Charleston, box-step and tango.   In my thirties, my friends in Lightshine, a church Singles group, (an off-the calendar event), would meet me at "Two Steps West", where we would country line dance to "Boot Scootin' Boogie", and "Achy Breaky Heart".   Back in the station at East Point, was not a tap-dancing time for Pauline, but she managed with her quick wit.

PAULINE:" A dude officer with his nose in the air stood by our car, only a cattle car, and remarked to me "Lady, I see you are on the way to hell! "Yes, sir". I replied. "I hope to open the gate so that such as you may pass in." A yell of laughter went up from the crowd. He sneaked off like the cur he had shown himself to be.

We passed through Jonesboro in the night. The moon shown bright and we could see the dead lying on the battlefield. It was a terrible sight.[8]

---

[8] A.A. Hoehling, Last Train. Ibid. Since the tracks were destroyed it was unclear exactly when Pauline left the city. The author's believe that she saw the bodies from Jonesboro as she stated, but it was after Sept. 2nd, it could have been from other cavalry skirmishes up and down the tracks. It is also noted that part of the trip could have been by wagon and then resumed on the railroad. It is said that there were many bodies that were buried by Union soldiers on September 2nd evening. This is probably the night she passed by.

Because Hood's army had fled Jonesboro, south to Lovejoy, there was no time to bury the dead. On the night of Sept. 2nd the Union soldiers were tasked with building trenches to dump the dead Rebels. Other wounded had already been moved to the hospitals in the area and beyond. There were 900 Confederates placed in a space less than 2 acres.[9]

CLARKE: 1980's "Passing Through Jonesboro"

Many a time I rode through the town of Jonesboro, home of Margaret Mitchell's original "Tara", past the square, continuing on Highway 138 towards "Indian Lake". My sister, Val, and I would go there often as teenagers, sometimes with friends, to soak up the sun, and take a dip in the man-made lake near Tara Country Club. One summer we went religiously due to boredom and the lack of something else fun to do, but I'd be lying if we also didn't hope we would meet boys there. We did meet a group of volunteer firemen; I believe my sister dated one of them. Even so, in the late 1970's, we never had a clue about what had taken place there over 100 years ago. Some say the Battle of Jonesboro was the turning point of the War Between the States that would end up deciding the fate of the Southern Confederacy.

PAULI NE: We arrived at Milner at 3 o'clock next day. We were set off the car beside the track—myself, three little children and a box containing all we had in the world.

Pauline arrived at Milner Station (later became the city of Milner) with her family, stepping out into a place she had never been before. At least she and her children had survived the horrors of War in Atlanta. However, probably unbeknown to her at the time, she had gotten off the train a few miles before

---

[9] A.A. Hoehling, Last Train Ibid. p 416-17

the site of an accident that had occurred before her arrival. There had been a horrendous train wreck on the Macon and Western line, on the tracks up ahead that occurred the day after the Battle of Jonesboro.

After realizing an eminent defeat, on the night of August 31st, General John Bell Hood, loaded many Confederate wounded soldiers from the area hospitals around Atlanta on a train heading south towards Macon. Also, that night, the troops were marching out of the city and, ordered to evacuate after burning the ammunition at the train yards to prevent use by enemy hands. It was a chaotic night. The train engine called "The Dispatch" pulled out of the Atlanta station, chugging along at 40 miles per hour. In the dark wee hours of the morning of September 1, 1864, the engineer, Bill Mitchell, had no idea that another train, "The Governor" was coming out of Macon. This train with supplies also included food rations and a car full of peas headed directly towards them. The Dispatch engineer said when he saw the Governor coming towards him, he threw on the brakes, but barely had time to take a few breaths when they collided. He stated "it was the worse wreck he was ever in".[10]

There was only single track in the area between Milner and Barnesville Georgia. Communications were non-existent and neither train knew about the other and they were approaching each other head-on! Ultimately and tragically, the two trains collided past Milner Station, at Lavenders Curve where it meets Canna Fax Road, killing thirty-one passengers instantly. Further injuries were added to the already wounded and weary troops who were being taken out of Atlanta.

Among the survivors of the wreck was a Confederate soldier who was "severely wounded" by a "Minnie ball" in the leg at the Battle of Jonesboro the day before the accident. Almost

---

[10] Engineers Account of Civil War Train Crash, posted by Walter Geiger in Features June 21, 2017.

30 years later, he wrote from Blakeley, Georgia to the Barnesville paper telling his story. He profusely thanked all of the women who rushed out to tend to the needs of the soldiers, but couldn't recall all of their names. There was also a letter from a wounded Union soldier from Missouri, who was riding on top of the train. He was one of 18 or more Yankee prisoners headed south. The destination was probably to Andersonville.[11] In later commentary on the accident, it was mentioned that there was one lady on the Dispatch train, who was killed instantly. She was a refugee from Nashville, and died within hours of the accident.[12]

Railroad cars being destroyed by Confederates before evacuating Atlanta

Confederate Prisoners Taken after the Battle of Jonesborough

---

[11] Note" 12/2/02 transcription by Lynn Cunningham/Pike Lamar County GA archives"Train Wreck in 1864 July 23 1891
[12] A.A. Hoehling, Last Train. Ibid. P439

Pauline D'Alvigny Campbell – Civil War Nurse

Confederate Prisoners Taken after the Battle of Jonesborough[13]

---

[13] https://georgiainfo.galileo.usg.edu/thisday/cwhistory/10/01/harpers-weekly-images-of-exploding-ammo-train-and-prisoners Images from Harpers Weekly Courtesy of Hargrett Rare Book and Manuscript Library / University of Georgia Libraries – both photos

Chapter 10: Preparing a Place (Fall and Winter 1864)

"Behold, I send an Angel before thee, to keep thee in the way, and to bring thee into the place which I have prepared." Exodus 23:20 KJV

PAULINE (now in Milner): "I saw a house not far away. On going to it I found Mrs. Dr. Willis Westmoreland in one room, Mrs. Dr. Taylor in another and Mrs. Gordon, mother of Mrs. Westmoreland, in the kitchen. Our Dr. Westmoreland of Atlanta, was a tiny baby at that time, and I camped in the smoke house."[1]

It was most likely re-assuring for Pauline to finally be out of Atlanta safe and sound, and in familiar company. She would have known these women very well through her father's work and the Women's society and various past social events. In fact, she even stayed at the Westmoreland home in Atlanta, as we now know was not a very safe haven. After the War was over it was reported that the Westmoreland home received shell damage.[2]

CLARKE: 2000's Sunday in the Park – Who by chance will you meet today?

"Sunday in the Park" is an annual event held at Oakland cemetery. It is a fun time, when there is entertainment, food and tours of the famous local "residents", including Bobby Jones, Margaret Mitchell and Atlanta Mayor Maynard Jackson. There are several plaques at the cemetery regarding the Civil War, about the "Great Locomotive Chase" where the Raiders were hung, and a plaque that states where Hood stood as he

---

[1] Note on Pauline's account. The Westmoreland's had a son named Willis who was a child during the War. No information has been found yet regarding Dr. Taylor and his family.

[2] Thomas Martin, "Atlanta and It's Buildings", 1902 p. 502

watched the Battle of Atlanta. It is usually very crowded with a few people dressing up in period outfits for the Victorian costume contest. By far the strangest day, was when we saw a parade of "Zombies", hundreds of them marching through the park. This was not planned and very unexpected, but it is a public park, and the organizers could not stop them. There was some type of Zombie convention or filming in Atlanta that day. They decided all at once to converge upon the park and parade around. It was quite a spectacle, hopefully to not scare children as this is a family-friendly place.

Rick and I typically attend the celebration at Oakland each year at Dr. D'Alvigny's gravesite. We dress up in our period attire and greet people interested in the D'Alvigny family that stop by. We have met many interesting folk, from around town and some just visiting. We set up a table and on one occasion we had Pauline's picture out (the one as a young woman) and a lady came up and told us she had seen another picture of Pauline at the Old Jail Museum in Barnesville.

Excited about this news, as we had only known of one picture, we headed to the Museum one day. It was a long two hour trip, and I insisted that we go through Clayton County, my old stomping grounds, which took even longer. Once we got there we saw a sign on the door, that the museum was closed for a family emergency. We were disappointed, but we looked around Barnesville, and also Milner. At the town of Milner we discovered a marker there that was where the make-shift hospital once stood. A house now occupies the space where tents were set up in a grove of trees.[3] The hospital itself was a group of large tents, holding ten men each. A Tennessee soldier of the 9th Infantry, James Fleming, describes it as having comfortable cots and describes the place has having such "pure air" among the pine trees. Fleming was injured in the Battle of

---

[3] Mrs. Augusta Lambdin, Editor, "History of Lamar County" The Barnesville News-Gazette 1932 from Atlanta History Center p50

Atlanta and stayed at the Milner Station hospital in July, staying only a couple of weeks before moving on to another convalescence hospital. He had great respect for Dr. Westmoreland who was in charge, and stated, "this was the best regulated hospital that I was ever in."[4]

PAULINE: The elder Dr. Westmoreland had gone on to Albany to prepare a place to convey the wounded that he had charge of in Milner. Next day he returned, but there were 25 soldiers too ill to be moved. He left them in care of Dr. Hunt, Mr. Brown and myself. Dr. Hunt brought his wife to stay with me.[5]

There was a family of Hunt doctors from Milner. Francis Marion Hunt born in 1839 was a prominent physician who grew up in the area. A graduate of the Atlanta Medical College, he was instructed by the Westmoreland brothers. He was also the assistant surgeon at the Medical college hospital in Milner during the War. His parents were Dr. John Poleman Hunt and Martha Garr. John Hunt was a doctor, preacher, and one of the founders of the Milner Methodist church.[6] It remains unknown, which Dr. Hunt stayed behind per Pauline's description.[7]

According to the account of Emma Tyler Blalock, a teenager at the time in nearby Barnesville, the young girls dreamed of being a nurse, like Florence Nightingale. Enthralled

---

[4] James R. Fleming, "The Confederate Ninth Tennessee Infantry", 1996, 2006, White Main Publishing Co,/Pelican Publishing online Google books p 122

[5] Pauline's Account. No information found on Mr. Brown- presumably a civilian not in the war for whatever reason, and possible nurse.

[6] Mrs. August Lambdin, History of Lamar County, Ibid. p316

[7] Note: A plaque on the property states John F. Hunt was the doctor, however, only John P. Hunt and Francis Marion Hunt are mentioned in the historical books of Lamar County. Dr. Westmoreland was originally from around this area, and would have known the Hunts very well.

with the Patriotic and romantic notions, they sewed socks and visited the wounded in the tents, with gifts of flowers, delicacies and books. She mentions that a handsome young Missourian caught her eye, and they corresponded.[8]

During this time most nurses were men with many being former soldiers. There was a 5-to-1 ratio of male nurses versus female[9]. Phoebe Yates Pember, a Confederate matron in a large Chimborazo hospital in Richmond, Virginia writes about the role of women of those days as nurses or hospital workers. There was a lot of bias in the day about women not being suited for such duties as tending to wounded soldiers, being around the horrors of war, such as death and other things considered un-lady-like. Female nurses were up against a lot of opposition, even from her fellow male surgeons and administrators, as most of the nurses were men during the War. Many women, such as Pauline, stepped-up or volunteered due to the shortage of care for the wounded and dying. Their own need to contribute added to their husband's service out on the battlefields. On this subject, Phoebe states, in "hoping with those almost beyond hope in this world; praying by the bed-side of the lonely and heart-stricken; closing the eyes of boys hardly old enough...a woman most soar beyond conventional modesty...if the ordeal does not chasten and purify...and if the daily fire through which she passes does not draw from her nature the sweet fragrance of benevolence, charity and love, then a hospital has been no fit place for her."[10]

---

[8] Account of Emma Tyler Blalock, War Memories, History of Lamar County p240, 241

[9] "Women in Wartime, 1861-1865", "Powers of Endurance" by Patricia B. Mithcell, Chatham, VA, 1999 p. 21

[10] "A Southern Women's Story, Life in Confederate Richmond" by Phoebe Yates Pember, Edited by Bell I. Wiley, McCowart-Mercer Press Inc. 1954. P105

PAULINE: We had a scant supply of provisions and twenty-five coffins were left to bury the men in but we lost only one soldier. A Mr. Howe, put his crop of peas in the balance of the coffins.

As Head Matron of the hospital, typically with an assistant, Pauline would be in charge of the laundry, including receiving soiled clothes and bed linens, and sending them to laundress and then distributing them to the nurse. She was also in charge of the pantry and kitchen, reporting to the surgeon and preparing the proper diet for each of the patients, as instructed by the surgeon, and was responsible for the cleanliness of her area.[11] In this small hospital setting, and with her nursing skills, no doubt she would have also performed other duties as needed in tending to these soldiers who were extremely ill.

CLARKE: 2018 – Milner and Country Cooking

Per her account, Pauline had been given charge, along with Dr. Hunt and one other person to care for soldiers too ill or wounded to even move. It was amazing to us that they only lost one person. Instead of focusing on the impossible task of locating who the 24 surviving soldiers were, Rick and I decided to look for the one who died. So, we set out one day to possibly discover, who was that one person that they lost? A daunting task and it was nearly impossible to tell without extensive research. We headed out to Milner one Sunday afternoon. It happened to be Father's day. Rick's father Tom had only passed away two years ago, and my father had passed away in 2000 – both from cancer. My father's last residence was not too far from Milner in Hampton, Georgia that is near the speedway where they race cars.

---

[11] J. Julien Chisolm, M.D., "A manual of Military Surgery for the use of Surgeons in the Confederate States Army."Duties of Matron" chapter p 77

We had seen the plaque, noting the Medical college hospital location, but decided to look at the small cemetery mentioned on the plaque of the 108 buried men down the street – called the Confederate cemetery. We nearly passed it. It was on a small track of land in a triangle, basically in someone's backyard. We stepped out and saw the tombstones. In 1864, they could only mark the graves with stones or rocks. However we saw that those had been replaced with a traditional granite marker. I had a soldier in mind that I had found on the internet named John Duke of the 27th Regiment. Online records indicated that Private Duke (of the 27th Mississippi) had died September 19th, and was buried in Milner, so I thought perhaps, this is the soldier whom Pauline would have treated or known about. When we got there, there was no such name – Just rows and rows of gravestones that said "Unknown Soldier". However, there was one stone that mentioned the name "Private William Van Meter, KY". We later discovered he was of the Kentucky Orphan Brigade. We also checked the other local cemeteries and did not find any John Duke listed. Van Meter had died September 8th – so that was also a possibility that perhaps he had been wounded in Jonesboro where his regiment fought, and made his way to the care of Dr. Westmoreland and Pauline. We do not know for sure.

On the way home, Rick wanted to eat a specific dining place near the area with country cooking where you ate with strangers around the table while the waitresses continually re-filled the dishes with "all you can eat buffet". He had only eaten there once, and thought I would really like the Southern fare. We ended up eating with a family celebrating Father's Day, and here we were missing our fathers, and only being partially successful with our research trip. As we left, I suddenly realized that my Father, Ray, had brought me here years ago with his second wife, before I was married over 22 years ago. This was a great trip to honor our Fathers on this special day.

CLARKE: Fall of 2011: Southern Treats

Going on vacation is like trick or treating. You get all dressed up, venture out to familiar haunts and some new places. You hope you end up with lots of your favorite candy. My recent trip to Tennessee was full of treats – heartfelt stories, wise sayings and even a few surprises here and there.

My husband, Rick, selected Tullahoma, Tennessee as the place to stay on our three day vacation for several reasons. It is situated almost exactly between Franklin and Chattanooga, two of the tourist spots we were planning to visit. Being a railroad buff, he had discovered online that Tullahoma was an excellent hotel for train-watching. We had never heard of the city before, and were taking somewhat of a risk. Apparently some of the reservation agents at the hotel had never heard of the town either, as we had to repeat the name several times and spell it out.

Getting to Tullahoma was somewhat of a challenge. We got some bad advice, and ended up travelling a few miles out of our way. We went through Arnold Air Force base in a very rural area on less than a quarter of a tank of gas. No gas station in sight for a long time. After a few wrong turns, we finally made it to our hotel before dark, and our train resources were right. We could see the freight trains passing from our room. Lucky for me it was far enough away and the passing trains did not interrupt my sleep. In town there were a few antique shops, lots of retail and restaurant chains, and one local treat- all you can eat catfish and chicken. The waitress couldn't believe Rick ate five whole catfish. I loved their navy beans and onion rings. Goodbye to counting calories, we were on vacation! Our next stop was Franklin, Tennessee.

CLARKE: A Step Back in Time
Franklin Tennessee

The next day we visited Franklin, Tennessee. At first I was reluctant about going.   One of my quips that I often repeated was as follows: "if you've seen one battlefield, you've seen them all". As Civil War re-enactors interested in historical places, we have toured many battlefields and homes in our travels.   I was not sure what to expect in Franklin, mostly known for its Civil War battle in November of 1864.   Little did I know how much my opinion would change in the next twenty-four hours.

The night before our day trip to Franklin, I had brought along some old unopened magazines from two years earlier (still in the shrink wrap that I never had time to read).   I opened one up – reading the cover story about what at the time were the best cities in America in several different categories.   It was very interesting.   To my surprise they had noted Franklin as one of the top wealthiest cities in America, known for making a great historical comeback[12].   The city in conjunction with the Civil War Preservation trust was trying to restore what they could of the battlefield there, and even mentioned buying up properties, such as golf courses and pizza places in order to do so.   This boosted my spirits about going to Franklin, so I became eager to see this notable city, just south of Nashville.

Our first stop was the Carnton Plantation that was used as a field hospital.   Part of the tour included entering a small room where the guide told us this was where the surgeon did the amputations, and pointed to a small window.   He said that there were so many wounded, it was like an assembly-line. Operations were done as hastily as possible, and the amputated legs were thrown out of the window, hurled to the ground where they

---

[12] City of Franklin, TN website http://www.franklintn.gov/community/history-of-franklin-tn

piled up. And then I looked down where he pointed to the floor, and the huge stain of blood, still there from over a century ago. The Carntons donated part of their land for a cemetery to bury the dead.

Rick walked among the graves of the fallen Confederate soldiers on the Carnton property enclosed by an iron fence. Mary Gay of Georgia, visited Carnton years after the War, knowing her step brother Thomie died in the Battle of Franklin in November 1864, and was buried there. When she arrived, she saw cows aimlessly grazing on the grass atop the graves. It pained her heart to see this, so she raised money to build the fence, and gate to honor the fallen Confederate burial grounds.[13]

Not far from Carnton was the Carter house, where part of the battle took place. A cat named Cleburne, after a Confederate General who died there, greeted us. I saw the barn riddled with bullet holes, and then we toured the grounds and the home. In fact, one of the young Carter boys was in the fight, and he hadn't been near his home in months. He broke away from the skirmish and finally made it there, but he was shot along the way. He died in the basement where the family, servants and friends had gathered while the Battle of Franklin raged all around them. As we toured the area and heard the stories, sadness gathered in my heart. This was probably similar to the bomb-proofs or underground shelters in Atlanta where Pauline sought refuge in with her children. I thought about the dangers, the fears and the tragedies of the families. Finally, I got it. This was so very real to me. This was War. I had never felt this way, in all the battlefields and homes I had stepped into before or after this day.

---

[13] "Georgia Women Their Lives and Times", edited by Ann Short Chirhart & Betty Wood, Univ of Georgia Press, 2009, p211 as per sourced from Tennessee Historical marker.

WAR –November and December 1864

While Pauline Campbell stayed in Milner she left her father to face the flames of Sherman back in Atlanta. Like a scene from the movie, *Gone With the Wind,* Dr. Noel D'Alvigny was left with hundreds of wounded. Noel treated soldiers from both sides saving many lives. The Atlanta Medical College was saved from being burned when Noel played a trick on General Sherman's Army.[14] The good doctor had his hospital staff pretending that they were patients, and the troops did not burn the building as there was no way for the men to vacate before marching to the sea.[15] General Hood in November 1864 marched away from Georgia toward Franklin, Tennessee before the enemy could advance any further. Hood wrote in his memoirs, "A sudden change in sentiment here took place among officers and men: the Army became metamorphosed, as were in one night."[16]

Editor General Clement A. Evans in his Confederate Military History wrote about Georgians under Hood in Franklin, TN. "We will now describe the gallant but fruitless effort of General Hood to restore the fortunes of the Confederacy in the West. In the ill-fated army that marched into Tennessee under General Hood, there were four brigades of Georgians, and parts of two others. In S.D. Lee's corps were Cumming's brigade and Stovall's brigade. In Cheatham's corps were Gist's brigade...and Tyler's brigade. ...Gist was killed." Cleburne was killed and following the battle, Bates Divison was sent to Murfreesboro. "Olmstead's brigade, at Murfreesboro during the Nashville catastrophe, marched to Columbia, the barefooted and ill-clad men suffering terribly in the intense cold, and during the

---

[14] Martin Moran, *Atlanta's Living Legacy, A History of Grady Memorial Hospital and Its People* (Atlanta,kimbarkpublishing.com) 2012,6

[15] Michael Rose, *Atlanta, A Portrait of the Civil War* (Atlanta, Arcadia Publishing, Inc.)1999 126

[16] J.B. Hood,*Advance and Retreat* (Secaucus, NJ, Blue and Grey Press) reprint 1985

subsequent retreat fought in the rear guard. Their successful charge upon the enemy's advance near Pulaski on Christmas day, is remembered as an example of heroic devotion. "[17] Five Confederate Generals were killed in the battle of Franklin and the Confederate defeat that followed at Nashville ended Hood's final effort.

Rick walking among rows upon rows of Confederate Tombstones at

Carnton Plantation, Franklin TN.

[17] Clement Evans *Confederate Military History* (Atlanta, GA Confederate Publishing Company 1899) Vol VII:372,373

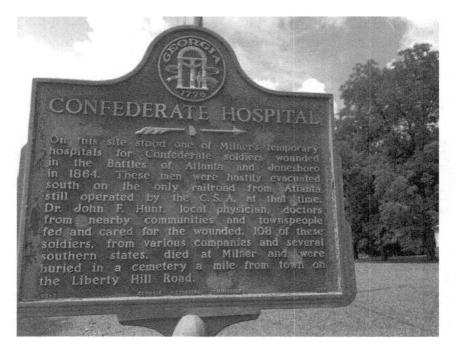

Plaque at site of Medical College Hospital, Milner, GA

On this site stood one of Milners Temporary hospitals for Confederate soldiers wounded in the Battles of Atlanta and Jonesboro in 1864. These men were hastily evacuated south on the only railroad from Atlanta. Dr. John F. Hunt local physician, doctors from nearby communities and townspeople fed and cared for the wounded. 108 of these soldiers from various companies and several southern states, died at Milner and were buried in a cemetery a mile from town on the Liberty Hill Road.

Pvt Wm H. Van Meter Co H 6 KY INF CSA

born July 27th, 1839, died Sept 8, 1864

Confederate Cemetery of 108 graves at Milner, Georgia

Chapter 11: 1865: To Everything a Season

"To everything there is a season, and a time to every purpose under the heaven: A time to be born, and a time to die; a time to plant, and a time to pluck up that which is planted; A time to kill, and a time to heal; a time to break down, and a time to build up; A time to weep, and a time to laugh; a time to mourn, and a time to dance; A time to cast away stones, and a time to gather stones together; a time to embrace, and a time to refrain from embracing; A time to get, and a time to lose; a time to keep, and a time to cast away; A time to rend, and a time to sew; a time to keep silence, and a time to speak; A time to love, and a time to hate; a time of war, and a time of peace." Ecclesiastes 3:-8 (KJV)

PAULINE: "Next January, our negro man came and moved us back to Atlanta, which he did in our own wagon, saving the same by going with Dr. Westmoreland from Atlanta."

After capturing Savannah as a Christmas present for Abraham Lincoln, Sherman's troops continued their march through the Carolinas. The Confederacy was in dire straits. On January 19[1] Lee accepts the promotion and becomes General-in-Chief to command all military forces.[1] Also reluctantly, in February, President Davis concedes to the calls of the people, and especially General Braxton Bragg, and re-instates the popular General Joe Johnston to command the Carolinas Campaign against Sherman[2]. Once again, the two foes fight each other. By mid-March his Confederate troops only number 20,000 while the Union has 100,000 men.[3] Pauline's brother Charles was in the Eastern Theatre in the Battle of Bentonville on March 19th thru the 20th, which was a Confederate loss.

---

[1] John Bowman, General Editor, "Chronicles of the War". World Publications Group, MA 2005 p.188

[2] https://en.wikipedia.org/wiki/Joseph_E._Johnston#North_Carolina_and_surrender_at_Bennett_Place referenced July 26, 2018

[3] Chronicles of the War. Ibid. p 196

In January of 1865, Pauline returned to Atlanta along with Dr. Westmoreland. Atlanta was considered the Western Theatre of the war. An update on Virginia, the Eastern Theatre is explained now.

In late-1864 through the first of April 1865, Co E. (Gwinnett) of the Leyden's artillery was near the James River, defending the line 8 miles south of Richmond near Fort Hoke and Fort Gilmer.[4] The Confederates were defeated during the Siege of Petersburg and the forces were retreating.[5] Lee had stopped to take refuge at the house of Kate Cox, whose family was taking in visitors after the fall of Petersburg. On April 2nd, the family entertained General Lee, as she mentions as noble and gallant. While he was partaking of coffee, she asked him if he took cream. His reply was that he had not had coffee in so long, he was afraid to take it all full strength. One of Lee's staff saw her puzzled look, and told her "you know the General sends all his coffee to the hospital".[6]

Robert was a hospital cook in Virginia late in the War. It is uncertain where Robert's Co. B was at this time. Richmond, the Confederate capital, was captured and occupied by the Union April 3rd, 1865.[7] Lee knew he was outnumbered and his troops were without supplies and food and it was over! On Palm Sunday, five days later, Lee surrendered. He sent Colonel Marshall to find a place for a meeting with Grant. The first civilian he encountered agreed to offer his parlor, Wilmer McLean. Ironically, McLean had moved to a house at Appomattox from Manassas, where the first Battle was fought,

---

[4] https://www.hmdb.org/marker.asp?marker=46915 – Historical Marker Database, "Fort Hoke Empty Victory"
[5] Susan Pendleton Lee, Ibid 333
[6] "My Confederate Girlhood, the Memoirs of Kate Virginia Cox Logan". P75
[7] https://www.history.com/this-day-in-history/confederate-capital-of-richmond-is-captured

to possibly escape war.[8] He had seen the first major battle, and was among the last to witness the beginning of the end of the War. After negotiations, General Lee rode his horse where he encountered his men. Several members of Leyden's artillery, including Robert Campbell were at Lee's Surrender at Appomattox Courthouse.[9] In cheers for their noble leader and at the same time highly emotional, as he passed by his men on his horse, Traveler. Lee then proclaimed he was proud of them, and then issued a final command for them to return to their homes.[10] The next day he states to the Army of Northern Virginia, "I earnestly pray that a Merciful God will extend to you His blessing and protection".[11]

CLARKE: 2012 – Appomattox Courthouse Scenes

Rick and I stopped at the Appomattox Courthouse in Virginia on our way to Gettysburg, Pennsylvania, while on vacation. We saw the McLean house and the parlor where General Lee and General Grant sat over coffee to discuss terms of surrender. We saw the spot of the famous apple tree, where apparently Robert E. Lee rested (according to the marker) while awaiting word from Grant about the surrender.[12]

PAULINE: "In May, my husband returned from the army, three weeks after the surrender. He had one shirt and his pants, and no money. I fortunately saved $100 in gold, and $35 went for a cow. We bought a mule for $80. Mr. Campbell put up a log hut, 10x12, into which we moved. I cooked our food under a tree.

---

[8] The Civil War", an illustrated History by Geoffrey C. Ward, with Rick Burns and Ken Burns. New York. 2005. P378
[9] Pauline's pension request form
[10] "The Civil War" ibid p 381
[11] Lee Wartime Papers, Vol 2 Robert E Lee from The Great Commanders, New York 1961 the Commonwealth of Virginia, p935
[12] https://www.hmdb.org/marker.asp?marker=30077 Historical Marker

I would wash clothes after supper and dry clothes by that night to have clean ones next morning."

The War did not end on April 9th, it continued on, and the Mississippi 27th surrendered on April 26th.[13] Robert finally made it back home. According to Franklin Garrett, Robert was in good health and not wounded.[14] It is said he would have probably returned on foot without any shoes, but was not in danger of capture after the surrender. He was likely given papers of a temporary pardon. Lincoln would eventually permanently pardon the Confederate soldiers, if they took an oath to re-enter into American citizenship. In the artillery unit, his responsibilities did not place him in the midst of battle, but toward the end of the War the Leyden's artillery merged in with the Infantry in the defense of Virginia. I am sure it was a happy reunion for Pauline and Robert and their family. Happy, yet tragic, as the aftermath of War, Atlanta was in ruin. Mostly due to Sherman's philosophy of "Total War", meaning War that involved civilians and non-military targets.[15] Some people were fortunate, but for the Campbell's, nearly everything they possessed was gone, including their house, and they had to re-build and re-plant crops.

PAULINE: "We borrowed the corn we planted from Mr. Clark Howell. A friend let us have two bushels of peas and another let us have a bushel of meal. We boiled the peas, at first without salt or meat. Our negro man got some garden seed from his wife for us which soon supplied a crop of vegetables."

A close friend of Clark Howell, and also a judge, exemplifies Judge Howell's character as being kind, generous

---

[13] R. A. Jarman, History of 27 regiment Aberdeen Examiner excerpt. No 5 p3 online version
[14] Franklin Garrett's Necrology
[15] Total War defined: https://en.wikipedia.org/wiki/Total_war

and fair. In the "Atlanta Constitution", shortly after Howell's death he gives a tribute to his friend: "No man will ever know the extent of his charities. He was always abundantly supplied with the world's goods and he gave freely. I know of many families that he supported entirely, just after the war and many a widow and orphan he has saved from hunger and cold and starvation."[16] Judge Howell's home had been burned by Sherman, but somehow his mill spared. In August of 1865, a few months after the War ended, he offered "to grind flour of any quality and any quantity at my mill five miles from Atlanta, on Peachtree Creek".[17] It was a time when community, no matter the age, status or race, came together to help out one another and recover from the devastation all around them.

One account of an un-named family writes to the London paper, that his father went to Atlanta from his plantation in Terrell County, Georgia to check on his house in Atlanta in December of 1864. He luckily found it standing, but mentioned witnessing the most "Devastation and ruin (that his) eyes had ever seen" after Sherman's army left Atlanta in the dust and ashes. He could only make it to Griffin by train due to "Sherman's neck-ties" where rails were twisted in all sorts of shapes. When he made it by wagon driven by 2 mules to Whitehall Street, it was barely passable with rubble, bricks and cinder filling the streets. Most of the businesses were gone, and few buildings remained. Many private residences had been burned as well. He also mentioned Dr. D'Alvigny had saved the Medical College which he was in charge of during the War.[18]

The reunited nation would now have one capitol.

---

[16] Atlanta Constitution of May 16, 1882

[17] David R. Kaufman, "Peachtree Creek, A Natural and Unnatural History of Atlanta's Watershed", University of Georgia Press, Athens in conj with the Atlanta History Center p143

[18] NewspaperArchive/UK/Middlesex/London/evening-herald/1865/02-13-pages-7 (Letter to Editor from C.A.L.)

CLARKE: Washington DC: Last Curtain Call

Rick and I finally made it inside of Ford's Theater. We had always wanted to take the tour, but didn't have a chance before due to timing. It was quite exquisite with the chandeliers, but not too grand, so that pretty much every seat in the house was a good one. Gazing up at the balcony where Lincoln was shot seemed surreal. It was hard to grasp that a former President, Abraham Lincoln, was shot and that it took place in this very building. Lincoln was assassinated by an actor, John Wilkes Booth on Good Friday, April 14th 1865.

We saw a skit performed, and once again replayed the story in our heads, that Lincoln had a premonition about his death, that Grant almost attended the theatre at that very showing of "My Favorite Cousin". And I learned that one of the stage hands had put a letter in his pocket, from John Wilkes Booth whom he had seen earlier that day. Booth had planned every detail. However, he could not have known he would break his leg and need medical attention. And he did not know that he would not be considered a hero among most Southerners, only a murderer.

They had a museum of the funeral procession and the aftermath of it all. Before seeing this exhibit, I had not realized how much the family endured, before and after his death. The tragedy would not end there. Whether you like or loathe the man, the story was one of sorrow. Abraham and Mary Lincoln had four sons, and three of them died before the age of 19. Robert Lincoln survived, but the family eventually died out in 1985, and there was no one left to carry on the Lincoln legacy. Today there are no descendants of Abraham Lincoln. Despite the last play ending in Ford's theater, the theater show would try to go again years later even in Atlanta.

CLARKE: The 1970's and 80's – Lights, Camera Action

The Senior Prom of North Clayton High school in the spring of 1979, was held at the (Fabulous) Fox Theater, based on Temples of the Egyptian region and originally commissioned by the Shriner's in the 1920's. I attended my Alma Mater's prom night, with a family friend, Stan. We both loved music and dancing, so it was a perfect venue to dance to disco hits of the Bee Gees, Donna Summer and Heatwave, in the elaborate and ornate Egyptian Ballroom. I absolutely love the Fox. Through the years it has held many special memories for me. After the prom, that summer, I became a volunteer usher at the insistence of Aunt Mildred, who was my great aunt and my Grandmother Olive's sister. A very active retiree, Aunt Mildred was special. She was the organist at Lakewood United Methodist church and the other churches she subsequently belonged to. Also, she was heavily involved in community affairs, including ushering at the Fox. Being very persuasive, she recruited my family to serve as volunteer ushers, but my sister Valorie, age 14 at the time, was too young to participate. Ushering was not difficult, just greeting people, pointing the way to the bathroom (which was down a huge staircase), holding a flashlight and hoping you were seating people in their correct seats. Since there was no pay involved, you actually had to "pay" by working lots of repeat shows in order to see a top-rated show. I saw some religious musicals, rock concerts and other events, (all second rate in my book), before being able to attend "Rick Nelson" in concert.

When Rick Nelson, aka Ricky, the son of Ozzie and Harriet of the popular 50's television show, took the stage, I was among the young and somewhat older girls making a bee-line to the front. Actually, I didn't think until later on, that someone might see my "usher" tag and wonder why is that usher running down the aisle with a camera in her hand? Shouldn't she be stopping people from doing so? Nevertheless, I got right to the front of the stage. Rick Nelson, leaned over with his guitar – looking right at me. He was a sight to behold for a teen, who absolutely loved his song "Garden Party" and had his greatest hits on cassette tape. I snapped a picture. Finally; It was worth the wait. Seven years later the musical icon would die in a plane crash.

Another great Fox moment was when I saw *"Gone with the Wind"* on the big screen, in its entirety, for the first time. On that day, little did I know that my future husband would be the descendent of the model for Dr. Meade, the Atlanta doctor, pretty much one of the few left to tend the wounded in that horrific summer of 1864.[19] Also, Tara was a name that I was already familiar with, from living in Clayton County (the very county that Scarlet's home, Tara was in). Tara Boulevard is the road I took to Clayton Junior College (now Clayton State University), and to a local mall, a hangout for the area youth. Tara was a fictional plantation, but modeled after Margaret Mitchell's grandparents' home in rural Clayton County. It was made much more grandiose in the movie, as the original family home was much more modest.

There was a movie theater in Atlanta called Tara. I used to work on the street where it is still located, Cheshire Bridge Road. Once I took my Grandmother Olive there to see a British movie, "Room with a View". Olive had been suffering from dementia and was at a nursing home in Union City, an Atlanta suburb. It was difficult to find movies that she would enjoy, so I thought this was a perfect choice as it was not rated, old English, critically acclaimed, etc. Will be pretty tame, I thought. She could use her walker, and it was all on one level, where she could easily enter, with my help, of course. When we got there, I pulled up close to the theater, parked, got Grandmother out, and slammed the door. Uh-oh. I had left the keys in the car. I

---

[19] Margaret Mitchell letters indicate that she knew of Dr. D'Alvigny and Franklin Garrett had confirmed this in person at "Ask Franklin" at Oakland cemetery.

decided to get her situated in the theater, and then I called a locksmith on the local payphone. This was before cell phones. Also, I noticed a "Tillie" machine within walking distance, so I could get cash to pay the locksmith. One of the original ATMs was called Tillie – I can still recall the jingle. By the time my keys were recovered, I had missed a good portion of the movie. I finally sat down to watch *"Room with a View"*, and man, did we get a view. Right before us on the screen was a bunch of naked men jumping in a lake. What have I taken my Grandmother to see! But, Grandmother seemed to be enjoying the film. Luckily, the rest of the film was a bit more modest.

Tara was originally owned by Loew's, the parent of MGM, where the premiere of *"Gone with the Wind"* was held in 1939[20]. At the premiere, a lamppost was lit. It was one of the original city lampposts that was struck by a shell, and later called the "Eternal Flame of the Confederacy".[21] Rick and I went to see it at Underground Atlanta, where it sat in its original spot that is now near Five Points Marta station. On the lamppost is a plaque, commemorating both *"Gone with the Wind"*, and a Confederate soldier and Atlanta banker, A.J. West. In 2018, the lamppost was moved to the Atlanta History Center. Dr. D'Alvigny will always be associated with the lamppost by treating the wounded Solomon Luckie.

---

[20] https://en.wikipedia.org/wiki/Tara_Theatre History of Loew's Tara Theater opened in 1968 sand Loew's Grand: https://en.wikipedia.org/wiki/Loew%27s_Grand_Theatre

[21] Plaque on the post

Pauline D'Alvigny Campbell – Civil War Nurse

Chapter 12: "Missing Beulah Land"

Thou shalt no more be termed Forsaken; neither shall thy land any more be termed Desolate: but thou shalt be called Hephzibah, and thy land Beulah: for the LORD delighteth in thee, " -Isaiah 62:4 (KJV)

PAULINE: "I am still living at the same old home and often talk over those hard old war times." –Mrs. Robert Campbell[1]

This ends the personal account by Pauline. Following is a synopsis of what happened to some of the people Pauline mentioned.

Dr. Noel D'Alvigny: continued serving as doctor working for the Union after the fall of Atlanta, and for the Freedman's Bureau at the Atlanta Medical College. The Atlanta Medical College was near the grounds of Grady Hospital today and is now known as Emory School of Medicine.[2] He helped save thousands of African Americans during the smallpox epidemic of 1866 and 1867, by giving vaccinations and raising funds. [3] D'Alvigney Street in Atlanta his named for him.

Judge Clark Howell: (Pauline & Robert Campbell's neighbor). After retiring as Judge, became the Postmaster in the Howell Mill area. He died in 1882 and is buried at Westview Cemetery. He was remembered for his generosity.

Dr. John Hunt and F.M. Hunt: (The Doctors in Milner)- John P. Hunt who was also a preacher passed away in 1887. His

---

[1] Mrs. Robert Campbell, The entire Account of Pauline is shown in bold letters enclosed in quotes, and was a typed on a piece of paper with no written date, in the Scrapbook of the "Women's Pioneer Society" housed at the Atlanta History Center, Kenan Research Library, Atlanta GA.
[2] Martin Moran, *"Tincture of Time, The Story of 150 Years of Medicine in Atlanta"* (Atlanta,Williams Printing) 1995, 33
[3] Cimbala,Paul A. *"Under the Guardianship of the Nation"* (Athens,GA University of Georgia Press)1997, 85

son Francis Marion died the next year in Mississippi in 1888 where he was a professor of Science. He had also became a preacher as his father and was known for his piety.[4]

Dr. Willis Westmoreland: Surgeon and Head of Surgery at the Atlanta Medical College and appointed as a General by Jefferson Davis. Dr. Westmoreland continued his practice after the war and became very well known in the nation. Having been co-founder of the *Atlanta Medical & Surgical Journal* with his brother John, he remained chairman of Surgery at the medical college, serving for 30 years. His son, Willis, Jr (the baby in Milner) continued his legacy as chairman of surgery. He died in 1890 at the age of 62 of apoplexy, unconsciousness or incapacity resulting from a cerebral hemorrhage or stroke.[5]

So what became of Pauline and her family after the War? According to her friend Sarah Huff, she and Robert were very happily married, and went on to have a total of thirteen children (twelve were still living as of 1923). However, her beloved Robert passed away on January 12, 1911.

Helen, Pauline's daughter was the middle child in 1864 in the midst of the War, among the three children she had with her during the ordeal. Helen married John Howell Bohler of the W.L. Bohler family who was prominent in the area. They had two children, a son Jesse and daughter Emma.

Emma married Milledge Horace Alexander, and Rick's grandmother Mildred was born in 1905, and had three sisters. Later when we asked Mildred, whose mind was fading, she didn't seem to remember her real Grandmother Helen. She

---

[4] Mrs. Augusta Lambdin, History of Lamar Ibid. p315

[5] Find-a-Grave https://www.findagrave.com/memorial/49467890/willis-foreman-westmoreland; A cyclopedia of American medical biography: comprising the lives of eminent deceased physicians and surgeons from 1610 to 1910 ...p494, 495 By Howard Atwood Kelly

would tell us that Pauline was her Grandmother. We pondered that something very tragic must have happened to Helen. It is not known what exactly, at this time. There is no account of her in the 1900 census. John Bohler remarried and moved to Cartersville.

Pauline was a member of the Mount Vernon Methodist church, which was founded by W.L Bohler.[6] The original church site is now occupied by another church, Collins United Methodist.[7] After the War, Mount Vernon Methodist had moved to Inman Yards. She was also a prominent member of the Women's Pioneer Society. Pauline survived Robert for thirteen years, and died on January 8, 1924. They are both buried on the family homestead, which is now a nice Buckhead subdivision. When she was ill, Sarah mentions that Pauline showed her some of the bullets that she had picked up while in Atlanta during the War.[8] The only marking on Pauline's tombstone is that of "Mother". That was certainly her calling in life, but to many other family and admirers, she was likely admired for her boldness and service during the War.

On July 4th, 1923, Independence Day, six months before her death, her friend Sarah Huff, wrote a tribute to Pauline, addressing the Women's Pioneer Society. She tells of her stories of the War, her bravery and commitment to the soldiers. At the end of the tribute, she states that Mrs. Robert Campbell, an 85 year old widow, is "enjoying the devotion of her children and grandchildren, and the love and high esteem of her many friends", who know her as "Pauline, the idol of the soldiers, and the heroine of the hospital".[9]

---

[6] Founder of Mt Vernon Methodist
[7] http://www.collinsumc.org/history/
[8] Sarah Huff, My 80 Years, Ibid.
[9] "Mrs Robert Campbell, ibid. by Sarah Huff

Helen M. Bohler was born in 1859 and age 5 years old in 1864

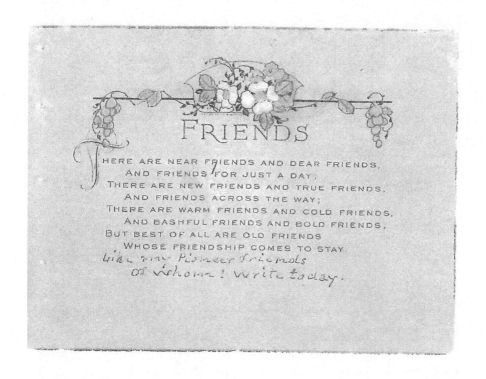

FRIENDS

THERE ARE NEAR FRIENDS AND DEAR FRIENDS,
AND FRIENDS FOR JUST A DAY;
THERE ARE NEW FRIENDS AND TRUE FRIENDS,
AND FRIENDS ACROSS THE WAY;
THERE ARE WARM FRIENDS AND COLD FRIENDS,
AND BASHFUL FRIENDS AND BOLD FRIENDS,
BUT BEST OF ALL ARE OLD FRIENDS
WHOSE FRIENDSHIP COMES TO STAY.
*Like my Pioneer friends
of whom I write today.*

*Mrs. Robert Campbell
A Heroine of the Hospital.*

(Source: Old Jail Museum, Barnesville Georgia, Poem-unknown author; writing by Sarah Huff in the Booklet of tribute to Pauline)

Pauline D'Alvigny Campbell – Civil War Nurse

Pauline D'Alvigny Campbell

Photo courtesy of family portrait in the Old Jail Museum, Barnesville